HANDBOOK FOR BAPTISTS

WHAT EVERY BAPTIST (NEW OR LONGTIME) SHOULD KNOW

BERNARD M. SPOONER
COMPILER AND GENERAL EDITOR

ROSS WEST
Publishing Consultant and Process Editor

In Collaboration with the Writers

Christian Leadership Publishing
Coppell, Texas

This book is dedicated to our daughters,
Joan Bush and Jane Carlisle.
My wife Pat and I
have been blessed to see our daughters become faithful wives
to their husbands David and Russ
and loving mothers to our four grandchildren:
Ashley Carlisle
Allie Carlisle
Aaron Bush
Alec Bush

— BERNARD M. SPOONER

Contents

Introduction

Over the years, I have observed that many Baptists have little understanding about their roots as Baptist Christians. My high school years and my freshman year in college were spent in an excellent Christian-based interdenominational school, The Berry Schools, near Rome, Georgia. It was not until I transferred to a Baptist college that I began to understand Baptists more fully as a distinctive faith group. In my college church, I was introduced to Baptist history and Baptist beliefs. We also learned about Baptist polity and organization and missions. This was an exciting time for me as I began to find a clear identity as a Baptist Christian.

Following college, I went into the military and was determined to be faithful as a Christian. My wife Pat and I joined the Service Memorial Southern Baptist Church in Oceanside, California. Soon we were asked to teach Sunday School. Pat taught the four- and five-year-olds, and I taught the youth. A few months later, our Sunday School director left the military, and I was asked to take his place. This experience taught me that I needed to be a better informed Christian and Baptist.

The Purpose of This Book

This handbook is designed to give church lay leaders, pastors, and staff members a brief ready-reference for helping new members, new Christians, and longtime Baptists understand what it means to be a Christian and a Baptist. The various chapters answer questions such as these:

- Who are Baptists, and how are we contributing to the cause of Christ?
- What are some basic beliefs of Baptists?
- What do I need to understand about my faith, and what are some spiritual disciplines I need to practice to be a growing Christian?
- Why is it important to belong to a local church?
- What are some essential things a church must do?
- Do I have gifts for serving God?
- How should Baptists relate to other Baptists and to other Christian groups?
- How can parents, grandparents, and others help children to come to faith in Jesus Christ and understand what it means?

Some Possible Uses of This Book

- Use it for teaching a new member class. Teaching procedures are provided in the appendix for teaching each chapter.
- Give each new member a copy, or place copies in new member packets.
- The section pertaining to children can be used in a new member class and by their parents as a guide for teaching their children the tenets of Baptist Christianity.
- This book can be used as a resource for Sunday School teachers or for those who work in various ministries of the church.
- Pastors may use sections of this book as supplementary materials to a preaching series on growing in one's faith.
- Use it as a resource for a special study, such as, "Who Are Baptists, and What Do They Believe?"
- Church members can use this small book to help their non-Baptist friends understand who Baptists are and what some of their basic beliefs are.

- Children's workers can do a study of this book to gain background for teaching in Sunday School or in other ministries of the church.
- Youth or collegiate teachers can study it to gain background for teaching in Sunday School or other ministries of the church.
- Adult teachers can study it to gain background for teaching in Sunday School or other ministries of the church.

About the Writers

Writers were carefully selected because of their long experience as Baptist leaders and their particular expertise. Below is a brief biographical statement about each writer who contributed to this book:

Phil Lineberger, D.Min., pastor of Sugar Land Baptist Church, Sugar Land, Texas; former president of the Baptist General Convention of Texas; frequent curriculum writer for BaptistWay Press®

Dennis Parrott, M.A. Christian Education; formerly director, Bible Study/Discipleship Center, Baptist General Convention of Texas (retired); veteran Christian Education leader and consultant; frequent curriculum writer for BaptistWay Press®

William M. Pinson, Ph.D., executive director emeritus, Baptist General Convention of Texas; former president of Golden Gate Baptist Seminary; Distinguished Professor of both Truett Theological Seminary and Dallas Baptist University

Royce Rose, Ph.D., professor of Educational Leadership and coordinator of Doctoral Ministry Programs, Gary Cook Graduate School of Leadership, Dallas Baptist University, Dallas, Texas

Thomas Sanders, Ph.D., director of Master of Arts in Christian Education: Childhood Ministry and associate professor of Christian Education, Leadership, and Research, Gary Cook Graduate School of Leadership, Dallas Baptist University, Dallas, Texas

Bernard M. Spooner, Ph.D., professor and associate dean, Gary Cook Graduate School of Leadership, Dallas Baptist University, Dallas, Texas; formerly director, Bible Study/Discipleship Center, Baptist General Convention of Texas (retired)

Michael E. Williams, Ph.D., professor of Christian History, Dallas Baptist University, Dallas, Texas

Publishing consultant and process editor: Ross West, D.Min., president, Positive Difference Communications; formerly publisher of BaptistWay Press®, Baptist General Convention of Texas (retired); veteran curriculum planner and Christian Education leader

CHAPTER 1

What Does Having Personal Faith Mean, and How Does That Affect My Daily Life?

By Phil Lineberger

In the late 1980s, my wife and I were in Interlaken, Switzerland, for a speaking engagement with the European Baptist Convention. Interlaken is situated in the Swiss Alps between two very beautiful lakes. The name Interlaken means *between the lakes*. While we were there, we watched people parasailing over the Alps above the village. My wife suggested that we go parasailing too, which meant flying through the air under a winged canopy several thousand feet above some of the highest mountains in the world. This was not something I had ever wanted to do. But after listening to my wife's suggestion several times, I thought it would be better to die parasailing over the Alps than to listen to her regale me with regret the rest of my life.

We drove to a site where we rented boots and helmets. After we were properly suited up, the instructors took us to the top of one of the mountains and strapped us into our sails. Fortunately, an instructor was strapped into the sail as well. The instructor told me to run as hard as I could off the edge of the mountain where a burst of hot air (a thermal) would lift us into the sky. This was a test of faith. Would I believe what this man told me, or would I back out? I was being asked to make a conscious decision, a commitment — a step of faith.

How Do Belief And New Testament Faith Differ?

The New Testament writers speak of faith as belief in action. One has faith to the extent that one lives out what he or she says he or she believes. James writes, "In the same way, faith by itself, if it is not accompanied by action, is dead. But someone will say, 'You have faith; I have deeds.' Show me your faith without deeds, and I will show you my faith by what I do. You believe there is one God. Good! Even the demons believe that — and shudder" (James 2:16-19).

Even though I couldn't see the air that would lift my sail into the sky, I had witnessed others flying through the air in that same manner. I knew it could be done because I had seen it being done. I was reminded of Hebrews 11:1: "Now faith is being sure of what we hope for and *certain of what we do not see*" (italics added for emphasis). Even though I could not see the hot air that would lift my sail, I believed that it would because I had seen it lift others. Faith is simple but profound.

I started running and praying until I ran off the edge of the mountain into thin air. And guess what? The thermal lifted my instructor and me high into the air where we flew like a bird for more than forty-five minutes. The flight was the actualization of my faith.

We are introduced to the actualization of faith in Luke 17:11-19, which records an account of Jesus healing ten lepers. Jesus told the lepers to go and show themselves to the priest according to the Old Testament teaching in Leviticus 14:2. Luke 17:14b records, "And as they went, they were cleansed." "As they went" was the actualization of their faith. They were cleansed not when they heard what Jesus said but when they *did* what Jesus said.

Faith is the mental and emotional capacity to trust or have confidence in something or someone.

Who and What Is the Object of New Testament Faith?

Jesus said, "I tell you the truth, whoever hears my word and believes him who sent me has eternal life and will not be condemned; he has crossed over from death to life" (John 5:24).

Faith is born in a desire to believe in something or someone. Everyone has a desire called faith. Some put their faith in an object, such as a statue of some religious person, animal, religious symbol, or even a favorite team jersey. They believe that having this object around protects or empowers them. With this object present, they feel more secure or believe they will be helped to accomplish some goal in life.

Faith is a word used to denote an action based on belief or confidence in something or someone. It is used inside and outside a religious connotation. A person can have faith in the stock market, faith in the economy, faith in another person, faith in common sense ideas, or faith in various gods or idols. Faith is confidence or belief in something or someone. Faith is birthed in a person's mind and can affect the emotions. We can have faith in good news or bad news and feel the effects of that faith in our emotions. Genuine faith affects our behavior according to the content of that faith. We can approach a red traffic light while applying the brakes of our automobiles and have faith that the brakes will stop the automobile. Our confidence, our belief, and our faith in the brakes cause us to apply them. At the same time, our emotions remain calm because we trust the brakes.

— — — — — — — — — — — — — — — —

Faith is confidence or belief in something or someone.

— — — — — — — — — — — — — — — —

Our faith must have an object. The writer of Hebrews reminds us of the great faith Moses had: "By faith he left Egypt, not fearing the king's anger; he persevered because he saw him who is invisible" (Hebrews 11:27). Moses' faith was in God even though Moses could not see God with his eyes. Believers put their faith in Jesus even though they can't see him with their physical eyes. Believers see Jesus with their spiritual eyes. Jesus said to Thomas in John 20:29, "Because you have seen me, you have believed; blessed are those who have not seen and yet have believed."

Believers put their faith in Jesus even though they can't see him with their physical eyes.

Jesus — his life, death, burial, and resurrection — is the source of the Christian faith. Jesus brought visibility to God. When Philip said to Jesus, "Show us the Father" (John 14:8), Jesus replied, "Anyone who has seen me has seen the Father" (John 14:9).

When the Scriptures speak of faith, it is in light of the God of the Old Testament who became visible in Jesus Christ. New Testament faith becomes objective in all that Jesus is and all that Jesus is capable of doing.

Biblical Faith Is a Gift from God

Before the days of Jesus, the faith of the Israelites was in the God who spoke through the leaders and prophets and who provided evidence of his power in mighty ways. For instance, when the children of Israel were on the verge of going into the Promised Land of Canaan, several of the spies sent ahead of the people gave a bad report about the size and power of those who inhabited the land. Their faith in their own ability told them they were not powerful enough to overcome the inhabitants of the land. But Joshua and Caleb had faith in the power of God to provide them victory over the inhabitants of the land. "The land we passed through and explored is exceedingly good. If the Lord is pleased with us, he will lead us into that land, a land flowing with milk and honey, and will give it to us. Only don't rebel against the

Lord, and do not be afraid of the people of the land, because we will swallow them up. Their protection is gone, and but the Lord is with us. Do not be afraid of them!" (Numbers 14:7-9).

This kind of faith is a gift. Someone or some event causes one to believe when he or she did not believe before. For the believer, faith is a gift from God. (See Ephesians 2:8-9. The Holy Spirit is the agent who brings God's gift of faith to the believer. See John 16:7-11 and Titus 3:4-7.)

In fact, no one can come to God unless God's Spirit draws him or urges him to come (John 6:44-47). When God's Spirit urges us to come to God through the Scriptures, another person, or through his creation, we are enabled to respond positively. Jesus said in John 3:16, "For God so loved the world that he gave his one and only Son, that whoever believes in him shall not perish but have eternal life."

In Romans 10:9-10, Paul teaches us what it means to "believe in him." "That if you confess with your mouth [prayer of confession], 'Jesus is Lord,' and believe in your heart [mind] that God raised him from the dead, you will be saved. For it is with your heart that you believe and are justified, and it is with your mouth that you confess and are saved" [forgiven of all our sins forever]. Paul refers to this in Romans 5:1 as being "justified." (An easy way to remember what justified means in terms of our Christian faith is *just as if I had never sinned*.) The term justification is a legal term meaning *to be declared not guilty*. Even though we are guilty of sin, Jesus paid the price for our sin and took our guilt when he died on the cross. He did this so that we could be declared not guilty. Again, Paul writes in 2 Corinthians 5:21, "God made him who had no sin to be sin for us, so that in him we might become the righteousness of God." It is not in ourselves that we become righteous when we accept Jesus as Savior, but it is "in him" that we are righteous.

The term justification is a legal term meaning
to be declared not guilty.

A good illustration of this truth occurred several years ago in Memphis, Tennessee. A motorcycle policeman was using radar to detect speeding vehicles. When a vehicle came speeding down the highway, the policeman pursued and stopped the car. As he approached from the back of the car, he recognized it as his wife's car. He was in a dilemma. Should he let her go or ticket her? He decided that since he was in a public place, he would have to give her a ticket. She was steaming mad and told him that she would go to court to fight the ticket. The court date was set, and the policeman and wife appeared before the judge. The judge declared the wife guilty and assessed a fine of $150. The policeman took out his checkbook and wrote a check for $150. Even though his wife was guilty, the policeman paid her fine. Even though we are guilty of sin, Jesus paid our penalty.

Even though his wife was guilty, the policeman paid her fine.
Even though we are guilty of sin, Jesus paid our penalty.

New Testament Faith Provides Justification

Justification—being declared not guilty—comes to us through faith in Jesus Christ and his death and resurrection (Romans 5:1). The writer of Hebrews tells us, "And by that will, we have been made holy through the sacrifice of the body of Jesus Christ once for all" (Hebrews 10:10). We are not holy, but we have been "made holy." Again the writer of Hebrews states, "Then he adds: 'Their sins and lawless acts I will remember no more.' And where these have been forgiven, there is no longer any sacrifice for sin" (Heb. 10:17-18). Jesus did everything possible for us to be forgiven of all our sins and be saved forever.

Jesus assures us that our forgiveness and justification are secure: "My sheep listen to my voice; I know them, and they follow me. I give them eternal life and they shall never perish; no one can snatch them out of my hand. My Father, who has given them to me, is greater than all; no one can snatch them out of my Father's hand" (John 10:27-29). If anyone, including the devil, could snatch a believer from God's hands, then someone else or the devil would be more powerful than God is. If that were true, then God's sacrifice of Jesus on the cross would not have been powerful enough to secure salvation.

— — — — — — — — — — — — — — — — —

If anyone, including the devil, could snatch a believer from God's hands, then someone else or the devil would be more powerful than God is.

— — — — — — — — — — — — — — — — —

New Testament Faith Calls for the Witness of Baptism

Following our profession of faith in Jesus Christ, we need to be obedient to Jesus in baptism. In Matthew 28:19-20, Jesus told his disciples to make disciples and "baptize" them. Baptism is a symbol of the death, burial, and resurrection of Jesus Christ. Along with the cross, it is a central symbol of the Christian faith. In Acts 2:41, Luke writes these words following the sermon by Peter: "Those who accepted his message were baptized, and about three thousand people were added to their number that day." Baptism doesn't provide salvation. Baptism is a step of obedience to Jesus and is a symbol of salvation.

— — — — — — — — — — — — — — — — —

Baptism is a symbol of the death, burial, and resurrection of Jesus Christ.

— — — — — — — — — — — — — — — — —

Biblical Faith Is a Guide to Spiritual Growth or Sanctification

Biblical faith is a desire to believe in Jesus Christ as Savior. It is a gift from God that allows us to believe. Faith is also a guide for Christian growth. Biblical faith is not a place of arrival but a point of departure for a pilgrimage of grace. Living in God's grace renews our minds and transforms our thinking from *having* to follow God to *wanting* to follow God. After Jesus comes into our lives, he equips us through the Holy Spirit to live this new life of faith. This is called *sanctification*. It is the ongoing process of *working out our salvation* — working out what God has worked in us (Philippians 2:12). Sanctification is done by faith (Acts 26:18).

Biblical faith is not a place of arrival but a point of departure for a pilgrimage of grace. Living in God's grace renews our minds and transforms our thinking from having to follow God to wanting to follow God.

Sanctification is a maturing process. When we first begin our Christian walk, we are like newborn babies. No one expects a newborn baby to possess the knowledge and maturity of an adolescent or an adult. It takes time to learn how to live life. We are taught to eat, to drink, to sleep, to exercise, to read, to work, and so on. In the process of sanctification, a new believer is taught to worship, to pray, to give, to witness, and to minister.

However, a person who has been newly born into the Christian faith cannot be expected to live a mature Christian life immediately. Everyone matures spiritually at a different pace because of age and circumstances.

A person who has been newly born into the Christian faith cannot be expected to live a mature Christian life immediately.

Paul spoke to the believers in Corinth as "infants in Christ" because they needed the milk of the gospel rather than the meat of the gospel (1 Corinthians 3:1-2). The writer of Hebrews encouraged the believers to "leave the elementary teachings about Christ and go on to maturity" (Heb. 6:1).

Sanctification means growing into maturity; it is a lifelong process. Paul wrote, "Being confident of this, that he who began a good work in you will carry it on to completion until the day of Christ Jesus" (Phil. 1:6). Paul also wrote, "Therefore we do not lose heart. Though outwardly we are wasting away, yet inwardly we are being renewed day by day" (2 Corinthians 4:16). Renewal and completion are products of sanctification.

The writer of Hebrews described sanctification with these words: "...because by one sacrifice he [Jesus] has made perfect [justification] those who are being made holy [sanctification]" (Heb. 10:14). The word holy means *to be set apart for a purpose* or *to be different from those without saving faith*. After a person expresses faith in Jesus Christ as Lord and Savior, Jesus begins guiding him or her along the path of sanctification using Scripture, prayer, and ministry with spiritual gifts. These are spiritual disciplines given to us by God for our spiritual growth and maturity.

Sanctification Is Accomplished Through Spiritual Gifts and Spiritual Disciplines

Sanctification is accomplished by the use of the gifts of the Spirit and spiritual disciplines. The word *discipline* comes from the word for *disciple*. Being disciplined means doing what we are supposed to do when we are supposed to do it. Being spiritually disciplined means doing what *God* wants us to do when we are supposed to do it. Only the power of the Holy Spirit can enable us to be disciples.

Paul wrote to the Corinthians that he didn't want them to be "ignorant" about spiritual gifts because "to each one the manifestation of the Spirit is given for the common good" (1 Cor. 12:1, 7). He then listed some of those spiritual gifts in 1 Corinthians 12:8-10. Other lists of spiritual gifts are found in Romans 12:6-8, Ephesians 4:11, and 1 Peter 4:10-11.

Sanctification is the process of becoming mature in Christ Jesus. A number of spiritual disciplines provide spiritual formation and maturity in Christ. Jesus spoke of the three Jewish spiritual disciplines as prayer, fasting, and almsgiving (Matthew 6). Spiritual disciplines are tools the Holy Spirit uses in our lives to develop spiritual maturity in us.

Sanctification is the process of becoming mature in Christ Jesus. A number of spiritual disciplines provide spiritual formation and maturity in Christ.

The spiritual disciplines of the Christian believer include public worship, Bible study, prayer, tithing, witnessing, and ministry. There are many others as well, including fasting, journaling, and attending retreats to grow in fellowship with other Christians and draw closer to God in a setting away from our usual surroundings.

The spiritual discipline of public worship keeps us connected to God and other believers in acknowledging the worthiness of God. Believers come to God because God, in Christ, came to them. Believers were created to worship God. Nothing else will satisfy the believer's soul like the worship of God. Public worship is not something that is done for us by others; we are not merely passive observers. It is something we do in the company of other believers. Public worship provides encouragement as together we pray, sing, and study God's word. Hebrews 10:25 states, "Let us not give up meeting together, as some are in the habit of doing, but let us encourage one another — and all the more as you see the Day approaching."

The regular study of the Scriptures is a significantly important spiritual discipline. We have the Scriptures for instruction and guidance into sanctification. Paul wrote, "All Scripture is God-breathed and is useful for teaching, rebuking, correcting and training in righteousness, so that the man of God may be thoroughly equipped for every good work" (2 Timothy 3:16-17).

Through the Scriptures, we listen to God. God breathes spiritual life into us through the Scriptures.

Through the Scriptures, God reveals his will to us. Before Jesus began his public ministry, he was led by the Holy Spirit into the wilderness to prepare. The devil met Jesus there and tempted him to give up his ministry. Jesus said to the devil, "It is written: 'Man does not live on bread alone, but on every word that comes from the mouth of God'" (Matt. 4:4). The spiritual discipline of Bible study helps the believer grow in spiritual maturity and in the knowledge of God (see Psalm 119:105).

It is through the spiritual discipline of prayer that a believer establishes an intimate relationship with God through Jesus Christ. Through prayer, we speak to God. Paul reminds us that we are to pray about everything (Phil. 4:6). Through prayer, God sheds light on his will for our lives. In Jeremiah 33:3, God says, "Call to me and I will answer you...." Prayer is calling to God. Prayer is not just a mental attitude. Rather it is a personal presence recognized in the believer's life. It is the surest sign of fellowship with a living God. The writer of Hebrews said, "For we do not have a high priest who is unable to sympathize with our weaknesses, but we have one who has been tempted in every way, just as we are — yet was without sin. Let us then *approach the throne of grace with confidence*, so that we may receive mercy and find grace to help us in our time of need" (Heb. 4:15-16, italics added for emphasis).

The spiritual discipline of tithing — giving ten percent of our income to God's work — was reinforced by Jesus when he said in Matthew 23:23, "Woe to you, teachers of the law and Pharisees, you hypocrites! You give a tenth of your spices — mint, dill, and cumin. But you have neglected the more important matters of the law — justice, mercy, and faithfulness. You should have practiced the latter [justice, mercy, and faithfulness] *without neglecting the former*" [tithing] (italics added for emphasis). In Luke 6:38, Jesus said, "Give, and it will be given to you. A good measure, pressed down, shaken together and running over, will be poured into your lap. For with the measure you use, it will be measured to you." Paul wrote in 2 Corinthians 9:6-8, "Remember this:

Whoever sows sparingly will also reap sparingly, and whoever sows generously will also reap generously. Each man should give what he has decided in his heart to give, not reluctantly or under compulsion, for God loves a cheerful giver. And God is able to make all grace abound to you, so that in all things at all times, having all that you need, you will abound in every good work." When believers share through tithing, they share their goods and are reminded that people do not live by bread alone but by every word that comes out of the mouth of God (Matt. 4:4).

The spiritual discipline of witnessing was given as the last command of Jesus before he was taken up to heaven following his resurrection. In Matthew 28:19, Jesus said, "Therefore go and make disciples of all nations, baptizing them in the name of the Father and of the Son and of the Holy Spirit." Jesus told all those who would follow him that they would become witnesses when the power of the Holy Spirit came upon them (Acts 1:8). Some of our greatest spiritual growth will come as we share the gospel with others. Peter wrote in 1 Peter 3:15, "But in your hearts set apart Christ as Lord. Always be prepared to give an answer to everyone who asks you to give the reason for the hope that you have. But do this with gentleness and respect...."

Through the spiritual discipline of ministry, we work with God. We are created by God to do good works (see Ephesians 2:10). With our spiritual gifts we share our faith in tangible ways so that people will see our good works and glorify God who is in heaven (Matt. 5:16). In Hebrews 10:24, we read, "And let us consider how we may spur one another on toward love and good deeds."

Personal Faith and Personal Practice Rest on Obedience to God's Word

Jesus reminded his disciples that a life built on the belief and practice of his words would be established on a solid foundation (Matt. 7:24-27). The Book of James states that the evidence of faith is in the works of faith. A person shows what he or she believes about Jesus and God's word by doing what the word says (see James 1:22-25; 2:14-20).

Jesus set an "example" for his disciples by washing their feet. He told them that they should follow his example and be ministers of the gospel as servants. By doing this Jesus taught his disciples that they would be "blessed" — happy (John 13:12-17). A servant's job is to do all he or she can to make life better for others — to free them to be everything they can be. A servant's interest is not in himself or herself but in others.

A servant's job is to do all he or she can to make life better for others — to free them to be everything they can be.

Personal faith brings each one of us into a personal relationship with God through Jesus Christ. When we believe that Jesus died for our sins and was resurrected to give us eternal life, and we confess that belief publicly to others, we are saved (justified).

Personal faith opens the believer's life to spiritual growth (sanctification) through gifts of the Holy Spirit and spiritual disciplines. Through the Holy Spirit, God gives us the spiritual power we need to live a godly life in the midst of this fallen world.

The faith that is required to bring us into the kingdom of God is the same faith required to make us servants in the kingdom. Paul wrote, "For in the gospel a righteousness from God is revealed, a righteousness that is by faith from first to last, just as it is written: 'The righteous will live by faith'" (Romans 1:17). We become citizens of the kingdom of God by having the faith of a little child (Matt. 18:3). We become great in the kingdom of God by serving others with the faith of a disciple (Mark 9:35).

CHAPTER 2

Why Is Belonging to a Local Church Important?
By Royce Rose

What Is the Nature and Mission of the Local Church?

Not a Building—People

Most Baptists have been taught to understand that the term "the church" does not refer to a building on a street corner, in a shopping center, or on a country road. We know that the church is people who are believers in Christ who choose to join together to be what God wants them to be and do what God wants them to do. The Bible uses many terms to talk about these people: *people of God, God's building, God's flock, the body of Christ, a new humanity, a family, the Bride of Christ,* and *a branch and vine.* None of these terms gives a full picture of the nature of the church. In the New Testament, we also see several models that describe more fully the nature of the church: *the called out, a building built on one foundation,* and, one of Paul's favorites, *a living organism — the body of Christ.* ⏋

— — — — — — — — — — — — — — — — —

The church is not a building.

— — — — — — — — — — — — — — — — —

Ecclesia—the Called Out

One of the words that biblical writers use for the church is *ecclesia,* a Greek word meaning *the called-out ones.* Baptists have studied the use of this word throughout the New Testament to create a definition of the church that helps us understand its nature:

> A New Testament Church of the Lord Jesus is a local body of baptized believers who are associated by covenant in the faith and fellowship of the gospel, observing the two ordinances of Christ, committed to His teachings, exercising the gifts, rights and privileges invested in them by His Word, and seeking to extend the gospel to the ends of the earth.
>
> This church is an autonomous body operating through democratic processes under the Lordship of Jesus Christ. In such a congregation, members are equally responsible. Its scriptural officers are pastors and deacons.
>
> The New Testament speaks also of the church as the body of Christ, which includes all of the redeemed of all the ages. *(Baptist Faith and Message,* 1963)

A Fellowship of Believers

My favorite professor, Charles Tidwell, described the purpose of the church this way: *The purpose of the church is to be a fellowship of persons who have received Christ and who are attempting obediently to live the way of Christ to work faithfully with Him to bring others to God.* Fellowship is a powerful word. It speaks of our commitment to one another and our desire to be together.

We have a common nature as *persons who have received Christ*. We have also chosen to be in fellowship with Christ by receiving him, attempting to live as he lived, and working with him to bring others to God.

The Mission of the Church

If our nature as "the called-out ones" is to be a fellowship of believers, what is the mission of the church in the world? Maybe your church has a mission statement that has been adopted to give direction to the work of the church. Some churches use certain Scripture verses to describe their mission. You may be familiar with one or more of these passages. If not, they would make good reading for you as you consider being a Baptist Christian: Matthew 16:18-19; 28:18-20; Acts 1:8; 2 Corinthians 5:18; and Ephesians 3:8-11.

The following is a mission statement that Baptists have used for a number of years:

> The mission of a church, composed of baptized believers who share a personal commitment to Jesus Christ as Savior and Lord, is to be a redemptive body in Christ, through the power of the Holy Spirit, growing toward Christian maturity through worship, proclamation, and witness, nurture and education, and ministry to the whole world that God's purpose may be achieved.

Like any good mission statement, it clearly states what the church *is* and what the church *does*. Within this mission statement, you can identify some essential things that the church must do.

What Are the Essential Things a Church Must Do?

The church as a body of believers is founded on Christ and empowered by the Holy Spirit, but what are the essential things a church must do? Are there a minimum number of activities a church must offer its congregants? Must a church have

17

meetings? Must a church have worship services? Must a church baptize its members? Must a church have regular Bible studies? Must a church participate in missions or witnessing? Must a church observe the Lord's Supper? What about having a choir or a worship team? Is preaching necessary? Must a church have regular prayer meetings?

There are some basic practices the church implements simply because of who we are (the called-out ones) and *whose we are* (followers of Christ). Your church's list of basic activities and other churches' lists may differ in some ways, but for the sake of this study, let's use the list from the mission statement under the heading above, "The Mission of the Church." It says the church carries out its mission through *worship, proclamation and witness, nurture and education,* and *ministry.*

> *The church carries out its mission through worship, proclamation and witness, nurture and education, and ministry.*

1.) Worship

The first essential thing a church must do is worship. Worship is a natural response to God's work in our lives. Since the church is people, worship takes place with people together and individually. It would be hard to think of a church that did not meet together for worship. The writer of Hebrews reminded the people "not [to] give up meeting together" (Hebrews 10:25). Worship is our time to sing praises to God, to pray together, and to hear from God's word. Worship looks different in each church, but it is essential to being "church."

The church should also encourage individuals and families to worship apart from the corporate worship experiences within the church building. Singing praises, reading Scripture, praying, and reflecting on God's word are all acts of worship that we can do alone, as a family, or in smaller groups. Can a church be a church and not worship?

2.)

Proclaim and Witness

Another essential to being a church is proclaiming the gospel of Christ and bearing witness to the saving power of Christ. In Acts 1:8, Jesus empowers his followers to be his witnesses where they are and throughout the world. There are two facets to this essential part of the mission of the church. First, we are to proclaim and witness verbally. In other words, we are to speak the gospel to those who do not know Christ. Our words are important, and it is important to share the Good News with those who are in our reach. Certainly, the one who preaches shares the gospel verbally; but, as followers of Christ, we should each be ready to share what God has done for us.

Second, we proclaim and witness through the way we live. This is a call for ethical behavior and actions. The way we live speaks of the One we follow. The way we live is the testimony we give to the world that there is a better way. Our honesty in all of our dealings, the compassion we show to those we meet, the way we treat our friends and our enemies, and the way we use our time, talents, and resources all proclaim our witness to the world.

Both what we say and how we live as a church and as members of a church are essential to fulfilling the mission of the church. No matter how good your actions are, if you never speak the gospel, you will not fulfill the mission. And no matter how well you proclaim your faith, if your life does not match your word, your witness will be in vain. Francis of Assisi once said, "It is no use walking anywhere to preach unless our walking is our preaching." Can the church be the church and not proclaim and witness in word and deed?

3.)

Nurture and Educate

Currency of the Kingdom.

Nurture and education are two sides of the same coin that are essential if a church is to be *the church*. This is the disciple-making process Jesus talked about in Matthew 28:18-20. The church is to nurture its members. Nurturing is an organic process; we grow in Christ. The church finds ways to help people grow in their faith. People at different stages of life and

19

maturity need various approaches to this formative process. Christ expects everyone in the church to be growing. Even conversion is spoken of in terms of "new birth. Once a baby is born, we expect the baby to grow into an adult. The same is true of the children of God.

Education is also a natural process in the church, and it involves more than just knowing facts. Certainly, the church teaches Scripture and Christian living, but real Christian education equips people to pursue knowledge and to grow in faith on their own. It equips people to sit at the feet of the Master Teacher, Jesus, and to grow in wisdom and faith.

It is essential that the church nurture each disciple in his or her spiritual formation and educate each disciple in the Way of Christ. Can a church be a church if people are not being formed in their faith and are not learning to be disciples of Christ?

Minister

The final essential action of the church is ministry. To minister is to serve, to do needful and helpful things in the name of Christ and through his power. There are many needs in our world. As a minister said to me, "Everyone is either hurting or getting ready to hurt." Needs and hurts come in every shape and size. People have needs that range from the most basic, such as knowing where their next meal will come from, to dealing with feelings of loneliness, loss, and abandonment. People's needs are not restricted to the size of their bank account, the color of their skin, the language they speak, or their level of spiritual maturity.

Over and over again in the Gospels we hear Jesus commanding us to minister to people who are hungry, thirsty, naked, in prison, sick, and alone. The church ministers by helping people, not because they are potential believers, not because they are potential church members, not because of what the church may get from them, but rather because they need help and Christ commands it. Can a church really be a church if the people are not ministering to people who are hurting?

Most Essential

Which of these actions is most essential for a church? *They are all essential.* They relate directly to one another. Without worship, our witness and our ministry have no power and substance. If we are not nurtured and given proper training, our ministry may be poorly done and our proclamation may be errant. Each essential intention is critical in making the church what it should be. Each is critical in fulfilling the mission of the church.

— — — — — — — — — — — — — — — —

They are all essential.

— — — — — — — — — — — — — — — —

These essential actions work together in the ministry of the church. Members come together to worship and to be nurtured and educated. These functions equip them to go out and minister to the world, starting with those closest to them. This is such a natural process that it is like breathing in and out: the church nurtures and equips its people and sends them out to do the same in the world.

We have talked about the nature and mission of the church, and what the church does, but now we need to address directly the title of this study: **Why Belonging to a Local Church Is Important.**

How Does My Faith Relate to My Church and to Its Mission?

Christ Established and Died for the Church

We live in a very individualistic culture, and so a natural question might be, How does *my* faith relate to *my* church and its mission? As you read the Gospels and see what Christ was doing as he went about teaching and healing, you will see that he was preparing a group of followers to be his witnesses in Jerusalem, Judea, and Samaria, and then in the whole world. He was preparing a church. He was calling out an *ecclesia* and preparing them to be the church.

When you look at the whole of the New Testament, you will see Christ in the process of preparing the church, establishing the church, sending the church, dying for the church, and then coming for the church. If you are a Christ follower, if you have faith in Christ, then that faith must be expressed through the mission of the church. Accepting Christ as your Savior did not depend on the church, but growing in Christ and serving Christ does depend on the church.

no church = no growth = no meat

If you are a Christ follower, if you have faith in Christ, then that faith must be expressed through the mission of the church.

The Church Is Christ in the World

We have already talked about the fact that the church is a fellowship of people who are in fellowship with Christ. Jesus knew that none of us could continue in our faith, grow in our faith, and practice our faith without the support and encouragement of other believers. There is no place for "lone rangers" in the kingdom. God deals with people in community.

Jesus knew that the only way he could bring in the kingdom of God was to establish the church, a living entity where people could be nurtured and trained, and could join together on a journey to minister to and to share the love of God with the world. The church isn't perfect, and Christians aren't perfect, which might be exactly why God chose this entity to accomplish the reconciliation of humankind to their Creator. The church is God's plan.

The church isn't perfect, and Christians aren't perfect.

The Call of Christ Is a Call to Minister

Baptist educator Findley Edge once said that the gift of salvation and the call to minister are the same. The church is the "called out." Why was God calling people out? It was to bring the world back into fellowship with God. So, if you have been called to be a follower of Christ—meaning, you are a Christian—then you have been called to minister. Likewise, as a called-out person, you are part of a local church and your ministry is the ministry of that church. Your ability as a Christ follower to grow in your faith and to accomplish the ministry and mission God has for you is intricately related to the church and its mission in the world. But do you have what it takes to be part of that mission?

Do I Really Have Gifts for Serving God?

The discussion that follows is intended to help you answer this question for yourself.

Corollary

There is a corollary to the statement, "If you have been called to be a follower of Christ, then you have been called to minister." The corollary is *when Christ called you to be his follower and gave you a ministry, he also gave you the gifts necessary to carry out that ministry.* This doesn't mean that you recognize your gifts, or that these gifts are developed as they need to be. It simply means that God does not call you to serve without providing you with the gifts to do what you need to do in your service to him.

Thank you, God

Kinds of Gifts

There have been many studies on gifts. You can find instruments and surveys to help you discern the gifts that God has given you. You will find various lists of spiritual gifts in Scripture. One is in Romans 12:6-8, which list the gifts of prophesying, serving,

23

teaching, encouraging, leading and administering to the needs
of others, and showing mercy. (See also 1 Corinthians 12:8-10;
Ephesians 4:11; 1 Peter 4:10-11.) None of these lists is intended as
a comprehensive listing of all the gifts of all time. Gifts are given
to the people of God so that God's mission in the world can be
accomplished. God gives the gifts that are needed at a certain
time to minister to a certain group of people.

Gifts Are Discovered and Developed in the Church

Scripture teaches us that sometimes your gifts are recognized by
others before you even see them in yourself. Let other people in
your church help you discover the gifts that God has given you
for the ministry that God has called you to. But also realize that
it is in the church that gifts are developed. Ephesians 4:11-12 lists
some gifts that are given to certain people in the church to equip
the people in the church for their work of ministry. You can rely
on those in your church who are gifted to nurture and educate
you and to equip you for ministry.

Gifts Are for Ministry Anywhere

Sometimes we do not recognize the full spectrum of God's call or
God's gifts. Many times churches only help people identify and
develop their gifts for service within the church. God has given
certain gifts to enable people to do various ministries within
the church. Gifts are given to pastors and other church staff for
their ministry. Gifts are given to Bible study leaders, deacons,
committee members, team leaders, teachers, and others who
serve in ministries so that they can accomplish their calling in
the church. It is important that the church recognize and help
develop these gifts.

But God also gives gifts for ministry in the world. Remember
that Jesus first sends us to Jerusalem, Judea, and Samaria (meaning, our local communities), and then to the ends of the earth.
For the Christian, every vocation is a calling from God, and God

provides the gifts needed to accomplish that vocational calling. Work is a holy act. It represents the gifts that God has given every believer to contribute to the world that God created, the world that Christ died to save. So the church also needs to affirm those callings and those gifts. Through a program of spiritual formation, the church can equip the schoolteacher to be the best schoolteacher God has called her or him to be. Through a strong program of training in how to live the Christian life, the church can equip mail carriers and auto mechanics to be the best mail carriers and auto mechanics they can be in carrying out their calling to serve God.

For the Christian, every vocation is a calling from God, and God provides the gifts needed to accomplish that vocational calling.

So, Why Is Belonging to a Local Church Important?

- The church is people, and you are one of them.
- Christ died for the church and for you.
- The church's mission and your mission are dependent on one another.
- The church's job is to nurture and educate, and you need to be nurtured and educated.
- You have gifts that the church and the kingdom need, and the church is a place to discover and develop those gifts.
- The church needs you, and you need the church.

CHAPTER 3

Who Are the Baptists, and How Are We Contributing to the Cause of Christ?

By Michael E. Williams

Contrary to the attitudes of some, God did not say on the eighth day, "Let there be Baptists." Likewise, contrary to the beliefs of some, Baptists did not begin with John the Baptist, Jesus, and the Jordan River. Jesus' disciples did not organize the First Baptist Church of Jerusalem, and Paul's epistles were not addressed to the Baptist churches of Ephesus, Corinth, and Philippi.[1]

On the other hand, the first identifiable Baptist churches to emerge in the seventeenth century did not appear suddenly and miraculously. Rather, the emergence of Baptist churches related directly to a resurfacing of the New Testament concept of believer's baptism and the voluntary church. The organized Christian church had submerged this concept during the centuries between the writing of the New Testament and the Protestant Reformation. In Western Europe, the Roman Catholic Church developed as the dominant institution in education, government, economics, social, cultural, and even military life after the fall of the Roman Empire. While believer's baptism still occurred when Christianity penetrated pagan areas in Europe under both Roman Catholicism and Eastern Orthodoxy, infant baptism became the norm, and the parish church became the religious center of European communities.

In the early sixteenth century, however, reformers such as Martin Luther, Ulrich Zwingli, Thomas Cranmer, and John Calvin challenged the long-held assumptions of the Roman Catholic Church. Emphasizing the authority of the Bible, these reformers also stressed the importance of salvation through grace by faith rather than the rituals and works-related salvation that the medieval church had emphasized. As the Reformation spread throughout Europe, another group of reformers who came to be known as the Anabaptists emerged. Notable because of their insistence on believer's baptism, these radical reformers urged Christians to jettison infant baptism and return to the New Testament definition of *voluntary faith* and church membership, which could only be achieved through *believer's baptism.*

While there is no documented direct tie between the Anabaptists on the European continent and the first identifiable English Baptists, there was great similarity between the beliefs of the continental Anabaptists and the first English Baptists. There were also dissimilarities, for many of the early Anabaptists held to a radical separation from the world, including adoption of pacifism, unlike most of the early English Baptists. Many of those Anabaptists who survived the intense persecution enacted by both Protestants and Roman Catholics eventually evolved into Christians now identified as Mennonites.

Notable because of their insistence on believer's baptism, these radical reformers urged Christians to jettison infant baptism and return to the New Testament definition of voluntary faith and church membership, which could only be achieved through believer's baptism.

As the English Reformation took shape under the leadership of King Henry VIII and his Archbishop of Canterbury, Thomas Cranmer, the shape of the Anglican Church remained close to that of its Roman Catholic predecessor. Especially during the reign of Elizabeth I, Henry's daughter, significant numbers of English Christians sought to purify the Anglican Church of remnants of Roman Catholicism. These "Puritans" desired to remove the last vestiges of Roman Catholicism from the Church of England. As the Puritan movement developed, it included some who believed that the English church could not be purified; thus, they urged their followers to separate completely from the Anglican Church. They desired to restore the church to its original structure as described in the New Testament. These dissenters came to be known as Separatists, for they desired separation from the Church of England and from the Puritans who remained part of the established state church at that time. The English government heavily persecuted these Separatists, so much in fact, that many of them fled to the Dutch Netherlands where religious toleration existed in the early seventeenth century.

They desired to restore the church to its original structure as described in the New Testament.

The First English Baptists

Among those Separatists who migrated to the Netherlands was a small congregation led by John Smyth and Thomas Helwys. As this particular group of Separatists delved deeper into Scripture, they became convinced the New Testament advocated *believer's baptism* rather than the infant baptism performed by the established state churches, as well as both the Puritan and other Separatist congregations in England and the Netherlands. In 1609, this small group took the momentous step of embracing *believer's baptism*. Smyth first baptized himself and then baptized Thomas Helwys and others. In less than a year, Smyth regretted his self-baptism and insisted that these first Baptists should have received their baptism at the hands of the Mennonites who resided nearby. Smyth's gravitation toward these Mennonites ultimately caused a break between him and his followers, as well as Helwys and those who agreed with him. Smyth died from consumption before he formally became a Mennonite, although some of his followers did embrace the Mennonites, who accepted them into their fellowship.[2]

Helwys and the handful of Baptists who agreed with his position used this occasion to return to England despite the fact that they knew they would face intense persecution there. Indeed, Helwys believed that it had been wrong to flee persecution in the first place. When they returned, they founded the first Baptist church in England at Spitalfield, an area of London. Almost immediately after his return, Helwys wrote the first Baptist treatise on *religious liberty*, called *A Short Declaration of the Mistery of Iniquity*. In this short work, Helwys boldly proclaimed that neither King James I, nor for that matter any earthly ruler, could dictate matters of conscience. Helwys went further to add, "Let them be heretics, Turks, Jews, or whatsoever, it appertains not to the earthly power to punish them in the least measure."

Helwys added fuel to the fire by sending the king a copy of the book and writing a personal note inside the cover. Shortly thereafter, English authorities arrested him and threw him into prison, where he died a few years later. Likewise, Helwys's successor as pastor, John Murton, spent much of his pastorate in prison, eventually dying there in 1626. While in prison, however, Murton added to the Baptists' growing defense of religious liberty by writing two additional works on religious liberty despite the suffering he experienced in the harsh Newgate prison.[3]

Helwys wrote the first Baptist treatise on religious liberty, called A Short Declaration of the Mistery of Iniquity. In this short work, Helwys boldly proclaimed that neither King James I, nor for that matter any earthly ruler, could dictate matters of conscience.

The Smyth-Helwys-Murton congregation established several cardinal Baptist principles. They practiced *believer's baptism*, defended *religious liberty*, and courageously braved *persecution* for their faith. Despite persecution, they also intensely evangelized and spread their beliefs. Baptist historian H. Leon McBeth states that within twelve years of their return to England they had established four other Baptist churches in England, and by 1650, there were at least forty-seven of their churches.[4]

As this specific branch of Baptists, ultimately called General Baptists, formed and grew, another group of Baptists emerged in England. Like the General Baptists, these Baptists also emerged out of the Separatist movement in England. Unlike the General Baptists, who abandoned the Calvinism of both the Puritans and Separatists, this new branch of Baptists retained the basic theology of their Puritan forebears and remained more connected with them during the English Civil War. They became known as Particular Baptists due to their insistence that Christ's atonement was limited to the "particular" or the "elect," unlike the General Baptists of the Helwys congregation who believed that atonement was "general." These Particular Baptists broke away from the Separatists of London sometime in the 1630s, although historians are unclear as to exactly when this occurred. It is certain that this branch of Baptists had certainly developed by 1638, and that by 1644, seven of these Particular Baptist churches existed and issued their first confession of faith. Unlike the General Baptists, Particular Baptists generally engaged more directly with culture, going so far as to support Oliver Cromwell's New Model Army in the English Civil War.[5]

Much in the same way that the General Baptists contributed to Baptist history the reclaiming of believer's baptism and the earliest treatises on religious liberty in Baptist history, the Particular Baptists also made their own contributions to Baptist and Christian life. Particular Baptists were the first Baptists to recapture *believer's baptism by immersion* as the New Testament mode of baptism. Prior to this time, the General Baptists had most likely practiced baptism by pouring. Particular Baptists most likely reclaimed *believer's baptism by immersion* by the early 1640s and included this as the norm for Baptists by their first *confession of faith* issued in 1644. This confession, the London Confession of Faith 1644, became representative of another contribution of the Particular Baptist tradition.

While the General Baptists also issued *confessions of faith* rather than creeds like those of the Puritans and the Church of England that enforced conformity, the Particular Baptists placed even greater significance on confessions than did the General Baptists. Furthermore, while the General Baptists emphasized the importance of Scripture as the final authority for the church, Particular Baptists placed even greater emphasis on *scriptural authority* for their churches. Repeatedly, Particular Baptist confessions stressed authority of Scripture over traditions, creeds, and edicts.

The emphasis on *scriptural authority* has continued to be the cornerstone of Baptist thought throughout four centuries of Baptist life.[6] It has also led to a key principle rooted deep in the Baptist character, that of *freedom of conscience*. Baptists have historically believed that each believer has the *freedom of conscience* to interpret Scripture in his or her own way and to follow that interpretation of Scripture within the dictates of conscience. However, that *freedom of conscience* is to be tempered by active involvement in a local church congregation and within the broad boundaries of agreement to a *confession of faith*. Freedom of conscience and *scriptural authority* are also closely aligned with belief in *religious liberty* and the *separation of church and state*.

> *Freedom of conscience and scriptural authority are closely aligned with the belief in religious liberty and the separation of church and state.*

Baptists in America

About the same time that Particular Baptists were beginning to consider baptism by immersion and issue their first confession of faith, the first Baptists in America began to emerge. Like their English brothers and sisters, they also developed out of Puritanism and Separatism. Roger Williams, who fled England due to religious persecution, migrated to Massachusetts in 1630. Already a committed Separatist, Williams quickly angered the Puritan leaders in the Massachusetts Bay Colony. Advancing radical ideas such as the necessity of complete separation from the Church of England, separation of church and state, religious liberty for everyone, the practice of political democracy, and the especially radical concept that the Native Americans should be paid for their land, Williams found himself being tried by the Puritan courts of Massachusetts. Eventually exiled from Massachusetts in the dead of winter, Williams was rescued by the Native Americans he had befriended and for whom he served as an advocate. With the help of friends, Williams purchased land from the Native Americans and named his new colony Providence Plantations in what became the Rhode Island colony. Roger Williams managed to implement full *religious liberty* and *separation of church and state,* which extended even to those with whom he disagreed. Prior to establishing Providence and continuing afterward, he served as one of the earliest Protestant missionaries to the Native Americans in North America.[7]

One of the earliest actions that Williams took once he established Providence was to become involved in the creation of the First Baptist Church in America. While Williams left his Baptist faith behind and became a Seeker only a short time later, this church became not only the first Baptist church but also one of the most important in colonial America. Throughout his long life, Williams continued to defend *religious liberty* and *freedom of conscience.* In this endeavor, he partnered with an even more important colonial Baptist leader, also an early resident of Rhode Island, John Clarke.

While Williams left his Baptist faith behind and became a Seeker only a short time later, this church became not only the first Baptist church but also one of the most important in colonial America.

Clarke's pilgrimage to Baptist life was similar to that of Williams, but unlike Williams, Clarke remained a Baptist for the remainder of his life. In many ways, Smyth and Williams were considerably alike—they were both dynamic and creative figures willing to take on the establishment and attack conventional ideas, and they were intellectually and spiritually on the move. Clarke was more like Helwys. Clarke was a builder. This is not to say that Clarke compromised his values. Rather, Clarke held steadfastly to his Baptist convictions even as he defended many of the groundbreaking concepts that Williams also advocated. Clarke's work, *Ill Newes from New England*, became one of the earliest writings in American history to advocate *religious liberty*. Like Smyth, Helwys, Murton, and Williams, Clarke insisted upon *voluntarism* in religion. As Baptist historian Walter Shurden suggests, "The voluntary principle is the core value of Baptist people." It has continued to be one of the foundational ideas of Baptists throughout the centuries.[8]

Baptists in colonial America remained a relatively small and oppressed group throughout the first century of colonial life. However, in the mid-eighteenth century, perhaps no denomination benefitted more from the Great Awakening that spread throughout the colonies in those decades than the Baptists, even though the Awakening did not originate in Baptist churches. The primary leaders of the movement were Jonathan Edwards, a Congregationalist minister, and George Whitefield, an Anglican minister. As an increasing number of Congregationalists experienced renewed faith and dramatic conversions, however, many of them gravitated toward the New Light Congregationalist churches that embraced the ideas of the Awakening. Then, as these New Light Congregationalists studied the Bible, many of them adopted *believer's baptism* and became Baptists.

Two of these former Congregationalists, Isaac Backus and John Leland, became two of the most important Baptist leaders of the eighteenth and early nineteenth centuries. They are best known for being two of the leading Baptist advocates of *religious liberty* and *separation of church and state* during the revolutionary and early republic era. Three other former Congregationalists, Shubal

Stearns, Daniel Marshall, and Martha Stearns Marshall (Daniel's wife and Shubal's sister), became Baptists' foremost evangelists and church planters in the American South. Both Shurden and McBeth regard the first church they founded in North Carolina, the Sandy Creek Baptist Church, as one of the mother congregations of Southern Baptists.

Due to people like Backus, Leland, Stearns, and the Marshalls, Baptists exploded with growth in America during the colonial period. The influence of the Great Awakening and its aftermath also demonstrate another key contribution to the cause of Christ—that of intense evangelism Baptists, despite having their roots in the soil of heavy persecution, have consistently been a people deeply devoted to sharing their faith with others.

As these New Light Congregationalists studied the Bible, many of them adopted believer's baptism and became Baptists.

Baptists and the Modern Missions Movement

This passion for sharing the gospel also translated into another Baptist contribution to Christianity, that of Baptists' fervent *support of missions*. While British Baptists Andrew Fuller and William Carey are often regarded as the founders of the modern missions movement, Baptist interest in missions preceded these two missions giants. As noted previously, Roger Williams might well be labeled a pioneer missionary to the Native Americans of North America. Baptists' intense evangelism manifested itself in what might be called "home missions," and in the years during and after the American Revolution, former slave preacher David George carried Baptist missions to Nova Scotia. Later, George founded the nation of Sierra Leone and planted the first Baptist church in West Africa there in 1793.[10]

This passion for sharing the gospel also translated into another Baptist contribution to Christianity—that of Baptists' fervent *support of missions*

The best known and perhaps most important pioneers in the modern missions movement were the British Baptists Andrew Fuller and William Carey. Rejecting the hyper-Calvinism of British Baptists of the late eighteenth century and moved by the evangelical awakenings taking place in Britain and America, Fuller, Carey, and other Baptist pastors founded the Baptist Missionary Society and commissioned Carey to go to India. In a few years, Joshua Marshman and William Ward joined Carey in India and established the Serampore Mission. Fuller published his work, *The Gospel Worthy of All Acceptation* (1781), and Carey published his *An Enquiry* (1792), each of which explained their views concerning the biblical and theological reasons for Baptists fulfilling the Great Commission. Fuller's great sacrifice in devoting himself to supporting Carey's work in India and Carey's persistent efforts radically transformed the Baptist vision into one that became truly worldwide.

Subsequently in America, Luther Rice along with Ann and Adoniram Judson felt compelled to begin their own missions endeavors, which ultimately led to Baptists in America being equally committed to cooperative efforts to send missionaries worldwide. Not only did the General Missionary Conference in America support the Judsons' work in Burma, but they also undergirded the work of Gerhard Oncken, who became known as the "father of Continental Baptists." *Cooperative support of missions* ultimately became one of the pillars of Baptist life. In the years that followed, Baptist missionaries laid foundations of Baptist work that persists today, including Lott Cary, black Baptist pioneer missionary to Liberia, Charlotte "Lottie" Moon, missionary to China, and William and Anne Luther Bagby, missionaries to Brazil.[11]

Baptists and Education

Rooted in Baptists' belief in *freedom of conscience* has been a deep Baptist commitment to education. Although some Baptists have been suspicious of "too much" education as a damper on zealous evangelism, or they've been suspicious of higher education because of its associations with the established church in England or in Puritan New England, many Baptists also recognized the need for *cooperative support of higher education.* This was especially true in England and in the colonies prior to the creation of the United States. Institutions of higher education forbade dissenters from matriculating, or as McBeth writes, "Baptists faced harassment and second-class treatment at these schools," and "many were proselyted to the state religion before graduation." Therefore, Baptists found it imperative to begin institutions of higher education, especially for the intellectual development of Baptist ministers.

In England, the first Baptist college was Bristol College, founded in 1679. In the colonies, Baptists in America founded Rhode Island College (Brown University) in 1764, eventually locating in Providence, Rhode Island in 1770. While Brown University eventually left denominational control and became an independent private university, Bristol College remains the oldest Baptist college in the world. These two colleges, along with many educational endeavors in succeeding years, have made a substantial contribution to higher education, not only for Baptists but also for generations of students who have served in a multitude of capacities beyond that of ministers and missionaries.[12]

In the colonies, Baptists in America founded Rhode Island College (Brown University) in 1764.

Baptists and Social Justice

Also rooted in the Baptist belief in *freedom of conscience* has been Baptist advocacy for *social justice.* Unfortunately, not all Baptists have held to the importance of speaking out for the oppressed. Despite the fact that early Baptist history was filled with oppression of Baptists and the fact that early Baptists were most numerous among the poor and the outcast, Baptists have sometimes been guilty of ignoring oppression or being the oppressor. One of the dark stains on Baptist life has been the fact that some Baptists have defended slavery and segregation, or have failed to speak out on behalf of the poor, the oppressed, or the immigrant.

— — — — — — — — — — — — — — — —

Also rooted in the Baptist belief in freedom of conscience has been Baptist advocacy for social justice.

— — — — — — — — — — — — — — — —

Many Baptists, however, have spoken prophetically and worked to minister on behalf of those who have been downtrodden. In Great Britain, Abraham Booth preached against slavery and the slave trade at the same time that William Wilberforce led his crusade to end the slave trade in the British Empire. The British Baptist missionary to Jamaica, William Knibb, led the fight to end slavery in the British Empire by speaking out against the evils of slavery on the sugar plantations of the British Empire, and he dramatically defended the rights of blacks in England as well. Both Booth and Knibb spoke out on behalf of blacks and human rights and against slavery at times when not all Baptists did so. In the United States, abolitionist Baptists formed the American Baptist Anti-Slavery Convention in 1840, and many Baptists in the North became active proponents of immediate abolition of slavery in the American South. Unfortunately, slavery played a key role in the development of the Southern Baptist Convention in 1845, as most of the greatest Southern Baptist leaders supported slavery, and most Southern Baptists sided with the South when eleven southern states seceded and brought on the American Civil War.[13]

Baptists' fight for social justice did not end with the Civil War and the abolition of slavery. Especially as northern Baptists faced the problems of massive immigration and rapid urbanization along with a rapidly changing society, Baptists in America turned toward ministering to the poor in the East, who lived amidst squalor in urban settings, and the poor in the West, whose lives were entrenched in rural poverty. Baptist pastor and seminary professor Walter Rauschenbusch began his ministry in such a bad portion of New York City that New Yorkers labeled it "Hell's Kitchen." Rauschenbusch's experiences there led him to become a leader of the Social Gospel movement and to write the monumental book, *Christianity and the Social Crisis.*

Church historian Glenn Hinson describes Rauschenbusch's ideas in this book as a threefold argument. Rauschenbusch argued, "To serve Christ, [Christians] must try to construct a social order in which kingdom ways will prevail." He also argued, "Both the world and the church would benefit significantly from the recovery of Christianity's social mission. It might prevent the collapse of western civilization such as befell the Roman Empire." Finally, Rauschenbusch hoped "to persuade aroused Christians that hope lay at hand for corrective action...." Rauschenbusch believed that "the most important corrective is the spiritual regeneration that awakens individuals to their complicity in the sins of society and leads them to commit themselves to social reform." This advocacy for *social justice* became a key component of Northern Baptist life in the early part of the twentieth century, led in part by the efforts of Helen Barrett Montgomery. Montgomery also served as a key voice in seeking *social justice* for women, and she served as an example for women in denominational leadership. British Baptist pastor John Clifford adopted a similar set of ideals for *social justice* in Great Britain at the same time as Rauschenbusch.[14]

While some Baptists rejected portions of the theology that surrounded the Social Gospel movement as being liberal, other Baptists embraced cardinal elements of the movement without adopting all of its theology. Among Southern Baptists, Texas Baptist leader R. C. Buckner pioneered work among the poor, especially with regard to care for orphans. Southern Baptists Annie Armstrong, Fannie Heck, and others utilized the work of the Women's Missionary Union to promote not only *cooperative missions support* for both foreign and home missions but also to reach out to the poor. Some writers have labeled this more conservative brand of *social justice* advocacy as Social Christianity to distinguish it from the Social Gospel.[15]

Among Southern Baptists, Texas Baptist leader R. C. Buckner
pioneered work among the poor, especially with regard to care
for orphans.

Arising from the oppression of slavery and segregation in the American South, African-American Baptists have long been advocates of _social justice._ Pioneering Black Baptist leaders such as E. C. Morris and Nannie Helen Burroughs not only engaged in raising awareness of _cooperative missions support_ in the newly created National Baptist Convention but also _social justice_ issues. Burroughs scolded black ministers "for preaching 'too much heaven and too little practical Christian living.'" Burroughs also called on them to "make their religion a real, potent factor in race regeneration."[16]

This tradition of _social justice_ among African-American Baptists manifested itself most fully in the beginnings of the Civil Rights Movement of the 1950s and 1960s. Almost everyone is familiar with the Montgomery bus boycott and Martin Luther King, Jr. However, many people are not aware that the Civil Rights Movement began in the Black Baptist and other Black churches and was led by African-American ministers primarily. Everyone recognizes King as the leader of the movement, but many are not aware that before he was the leader of the movement, King was a Baptist minister, and his roots and the strong tradition of _social justice_ in the Black Baptist church contributed heavily to his early thought processes. Ultimately, the activism of King and others led to the creation of the Progressive National Baptist Convention to further support _social justice_ efforts.[17]

Conclusion

So who are Baptists, and how have we contributed to the cause of Christ? This chapter identifies some of the key individuals and ideals of Baptists across more than four hundred years of Baptist history. Despite the frequent, widespread _persecution_ that Baptists have endured in the past and continue to endure today in various parts of the world, we have always focused on and preached the importance of several key ideals. These are *voluntary faith/voluntarism; believer's baptism; religious liberty and separation of church and state;* utilization of voluntary *confessions of faith* rather than coercion or mandatory creeds; *scriptural authority; intense evangelism; cooperative support of missions and higher education; social justice;* and perhaps, most of all, *freedom of conscience* within the boundaries of a community of believers. Baptists have historically been freedom-loving people, and these key ideas represent that passion. While some of these concepts are not exclusive to Baptists, together they form the contributions that Baptists have made to Christian life and to the cause of Christ in the world.

Suggested Reading

Pam R. Durso and Keith E. Durso. *The Story of Baptists in the United States.* Brentwood, TN: The Baptist History and Heritage Society, 2006.

H. Leon McBeth. *The Baptist Heritage: Four Centuries of Baptist Witness.* Nashville: Broadman Press, 1987.

H. Leon McBeth. *A Sourcebook for Baptist Heritage.* Nashville: Broadman Press, 1990.

Michael E. Williams, Sr., and Walter B. Shurden, eds. *Turning Points in Baptist History.* Macon, GA: Mercer University Press, 2008.

CHAPTER 4

What Are Some Basic Baptist Beliefs?
By William M. Pinson

The Baptist denomination is part of the religious faith group known as Christianity. Therefore, Baptists have much in common with the beliefs that are basic to the Christian faith. However, Baptists are a distinctive part of the Christian movement, and as such, hold beliefs that set them apart from other denominations. This chapter is in two parts: (1) beliefs that Baptists hold in common with other Christians and (2) beliefs and practices that make Baptists a distinct denomination.

Beliefs Baptists Hold in Common with Other Christians

Baptists hold beliefs about God, Jesus Christ, humankind, salvation, the Bible, and church that are similar in many ways to those held by Christians in general. An abundance of information is available about these basic beliefs. What is offered here is but a very brief summary.

Belief about God

Baptists and other Christians believe there is one God. God creates and sustains all that exists. God is infinite, which means he is without limit. He is eternal, all-powerful, all knowing, and present everywhere at all times. God is holy and without fault; he is righteous, pure, and just. God is not an impersonal force incapable of having a relationship with human beings. He is a loving Father who desires fellowship with his children.

The Trinity is also one of the most basic Christian beliefs about God. God is three in one: Father, Son, and Holy Spirit. This does not mean that there are three Gods, but that in some way beyond human understanding, these three persons are also one.

Belief about Jesus Christ

The life and teachings of Jesus Christ are of utmost importance to Christians. Five words are often used to summarize the Christian belief in Jesus: *incarnation, crucifixion, resurrection, ascension,* and *parousia.*

Incarnation literally means "being in flesh." Christians believe that God was in Christ. Jesus was both fully human and fully divine. As such, he experienced human conditions such as thirst, weariness, and compassion. He also experienced all of the temptations that we do, but he remained without sin. His example and teachings have divine authority.

Incarnation literally means "being in flesh." Christians believe that God was in Christ. Jesus was both fully human and fully divine.

Crucifixion literally means "fixed to a cross." Although Christians have various views about how Jesus' death on the cross brought the hope of salvation to humankind, they agree that by his voluntary sacrifice on the cross, he made forgiveness of our sins possible through faith in him. As such, Jesus is our Redeemer!

Resurrection literally means "coming alive again." After his spirit departed from him, Jesus was taken from the cross by his friends and placed in a borrowed tomb. A huge stone was placed at the entrance, and thus the tomb was sealed. In three days, Jesus rose from the dead, and angels rolled away the stone. They did not have to remove the stone to allow Jesus to get out of the tomb, because his resurrected body could move through solid walls anyway. Rather, the angels moved the stone to allow anyone who came to the tomb to see inside it and know that Jesus was no longer there. He was alive! He had overcome death, and in doing so, his promise of eternal life to all who believed in him was valid and proven true.

Ascension literally means "going up." Following his resurrection, Jesus spent several days teaching and encouraging his disciples. Then one day he gave his final instructions (while on earth) to his disciples and ascended to heaven as they watched him go. No gravesite exists for Jesus. The Bible indicates that he is in heaven making intercession for us.

Parousia is from a Greek word meaning "presence." Jesus will be visibly present on earth again one day. Although Christians have various views on exactly when Christ's return will be and what it will mean for all of humanity, almost all agree that he is coming again in a very special way, and it will be a time of rejoicing for those who have trusted in him as Lord and Savior.

Although Christians have various views on exactly when Christ's return will be and what it will mean for all of humanity, almost all agree that he is coming again....

Belief about Humankind

Christians believe that human beings are part of God's creation — a very special part. God created humankind in his image and intended to have a relationship with us characterized by a loving fellowship with him as our creator. However, the first human beings, Adam and Eve, broke that trusting relationship by disobeying God's commands. God gave them freedom of choice; they were not created as puppets. Choices have consequences, and the consequence of their disobedience was sin and death.

The sinful nature of human beings is evident in multiple ways. For example, instead of worshipping the one true God, people worship many gods including idols made with human hands. They take the name of the true God in vain and live according to their will and not his. Pride leads to the concept that reason and human ingenuity can overcome the evil that lurks in every human being.

Belief about Salvation

Baptists share with other Christians the conviction that humankind cannot save itself but is in need of a savior. Although Christians differ to some degree among various denominations on how salvation is to take place, there is general agreement that salvation is needed and that Jesus Christ plays an essential role in salvation.

A common understanding among all Christian groups is that grace and faith are vital ingredients in salvation. Again, denominations differ to some degree on how grace and faith relate to salvation, but all denominations agree these two characteristics are essential.

A common understanding among all Christian groups is that grace and faith are vital ingredients in salvation.

Belief about the Bible

God revealed himself to inspired writers who recorded that revelation. The Bible is a collection of those records, and as such, it is a revelation of God. Thus, Baptists and other Christians look to the Bible for an understanding of God's nature and will, the life and teachings of Jesus, the condition of humankind, the need for and provision of salvation, and the nature and purpose of the church.

Admittedly, Christian denominations as well as individual Christians hold various views about the Bible, such as the nature of its inspiration, authority, and meaning. Nevertheless, all Christians look to the Bible as a very special book, a unique source of knowledge about God, Jesus, humankind, salvation, and church.

All Christians look to the Bible as a very special book, a unique source of knowledge about God, Jesus, humankind, salvation, and church.

Belief about Church

Jesus declared that he would build his church (Matthew 16:18). Through the ages, Christians of various denominations have agreed that church is a vital part of the Christian faith and life. A church is a community of persons who hold a common faith in God's provision of salvation through Jesus Christ.

Christians hold various ideas about the nature of church, who the leaders should be, how individuals can become part of a church, how worship should be conducted, and what the responsibilities of the members are. Yet all agree that persons who trust in Jesus as Savior and Lord ought to be part of a faith community, and the purpose of that faith community is to worship God, fellowship with one another, and serve the needs of others.

In summary, Baptists and other Christians believe in God and Jesus Christ, in the need and provision for salvation, and in the vital importance of the Bible and church. Denominations of Christians came into being as persons who believed in particular ways about these matters related to one another in some sort of organizational fashion. So it was with the Baptist denomination.

Baptists and other Christians believe in God and Jesus Christ, in the need and provision for salvation, and in the vital importance of the Bible and church. Denominations of Christians came into being as persons who believed in particular ways about these matters related to one another in some sort of organizational fashion. So it was with the Baptist denomination.

Beliefs and Practices That Make Baptists a Distinct Denomination

When a faith commitment is made to trust Jesus Christ as Savior and Lord, certain other decisions must be made, such as what to do about baptism, the Lord's Supper, the nature of church, and other matters. Because Christians hold varying views concerning these matters, the way they are interpreted is what sets apart one denomination from another.

Often when people speak of denominations, they are referring to the organizations of a denomination. These organizations, however, are not the denomination; they are the organized expressions of it. When people relate to one another around common beliefs, they form organizations of some kind. For Baptists, these organizations include such entities as associations, conventions, fellowships, societies, and unions.

What are the beliefs that make Baptists a distinct denomination? No single belief defines Baptists. Rather, a combination of beliefs makes the Baptist denomination a distinct fellowship of Christians. Baptists have no official list of these beliefs. However,

Baptists hold in common certain beliefs which, taken as a whole, identify Baptists as Baptists.

— — — — — — — — — — — — — — — —

No single belief defines Baptists. Rather, a combination of beliefs makes the Baptist denomination a distinct fellowship of Christians.

— — — — — — — — — — — — — — — —

Baptists are not all alike — not by a long shot! Part of the reason for the different kinds of Baptists is that Baptists differ on the interpretation and application of the basic beliefs that they hold in common. Baptist freedom makes it possible for Baptists to organize around those various interpretations. When they do so, they do not create a new denomination, but rather they create a new organizational expression of the Baptist denomination. For example, most Baptists conduct their primary weekly worship on Sunday, but some Baptists believe that such worship should take place on Saturday. They form the Seventh Day Baptists. But Sunday and Saturday Baptists are part of the same Baptist denomination. The following beliefs are those generally held by Baptist Christians.

The Bible Is the Sole Written Authority for Baptist Beliefs

God is the ultimate authority for Baptists, and the Bible and the Bible alone is the sole written authority for Baptist faith and practice. This commitment was emphasized in a sermon that George W. Truett preached in 1920 from the steps of the United States Capitol. Truett is acknowledged as one of the foremost Baptist leaders of all time. In this famous sermon, he declared:

> The Bible and the Bible alone is the rule of faith and practice for Baptists. To them the one standard by which all creeds and conduct and character must be tried is the Word of God. They ask only one question concerning all religious faith and practice and that question is, "What saith the Word of God?"

49

Not traditions, nor customs, nor councils, nor confessions, nor ecclesiastical formularies, however venerable and pretentious, guide Baptists, but simply and solely the will of Christ as they find it revealed in the New Testament.

The Lordship of Christ

George W. Truett in the same sermon emphasized this belief:

First of all, and explaining all the rest, is the doctrine of absolute Lordship of Jesus Christ. That doctrine is for Baptists the dominant fact in all their Christian experience, the nerve center of all their Christian life, the bedrock of all their church polity, the sheet anchor of all their hopes, the climax and crown of all their rejoicings.... From that germinal conception of the absolute Lordship of Christ, all our Baptist principles emerge.

Soul Competency

Baptist leaders have stressed how significant this belief is to Baptists. Herschel Hobbs, a Baptist pastor and theologian, wrote, "Out of this principle flow all other elements of Baptist belief." Various terms have been used for this concept, such as freedom of conscience, soul freedom, and soul competency. The basic meaning is the God-given freedom and ability of persons to know and respond to God's will. This includes the capability of persons to understand and respond to the teachings of the Bible. The concept of soul competency is based on the teachings of the Bible, such as these: God has provided freedom of choice as a gift, choice has consequences, each person is responsible for his or her choices, and faith in Christ is a personal and not a group matter.

The concept of soul competency is based on the teachings of the Bible, such as these: God has provided freedom of choice as a gift, choice has consequences, each person is responsible for his or her choices, and faith in Christ is a personal and not a group matter.

The Nature of Salvation

Salvation from sin and death to forgiveness and life comes only by a personal response of repentance and faith to God's grace gift of his Son, the Lord Jesus Christ. Baptists insist that salvation is only by God's grace and through our faith, not by our good works. This belief comes from the teachings of the Bible, such as Ephesians 2:8-9: "For it is by grace you have been saved through faith — and this not from yourselves, it is the gift of God — not by works, so that no one can boast."

Thus, Baptists teach that salvation comes not by good deeds, or baptism, or church membership, as important as these may be, but only by God's grace through faith. In this belief, Baptists differ from those who contend, for example, that baptism is necessary for salvation.

Thus, Baptists teach that salvation comes not by good deeds, or baptism, or church membership.

The Priesthood of All Believers

Every person who responds by faith to God's grace gift of salvation becomes a believer priest. Baptists treasure the biblical teaching concerning the priesthood of all believers (1 Peter 2:9; Revelation 1:6). The New Testament teaches that the priesthood of the Old Testament is no longer necessary because Jesus Christ, the great High Priest, has paid the price of sacrifice for our sins (Hebrews 7:23 — 8:13). At the crucifixion of Jesus, the veil in the temple that separated the holy of holies from the rest of the temple was torn from top to bottom, indicating that no longer was there a barrier between humankind and God.

By faith, each person has direct access to God and needs no human mediator. Each individual Christian is free to approach God in prayer and worship and to read and interpret God's Word under the leadership of the Holy Spirit.

- - - - - - - - - - - - - - - -

By faith, each person has direct access to God and needs no human mediator.

- - - - - - - - - - - - - - - -

The Bible indicates that each believer priest is to relate to other believer priests as part of a "royal priesthood." Although each believer priest is responsible for his or her decisions and actions, each one is expected to remain in fellowship with and consult with other believer priests. Being part of a community or congregation of believers is a vital part of the Christian life.

Believer's Baptism by Immersion

Baptists believe that the Bible teaches that only persons who have personally made a commitment to follow Jesus as Savior and Lord, that is, to be saved by faith through God's gracious gift of Christ, are to be baptized. Baptism in the New Testament always followed a person's conversion and never preceded it. Baptism was not necessary for a person to be saved, but it was a way for a person to testify that he or she had been saved. Baptists do not baptize infants because infants cannot personally place faith in Christ as Savior and Lord.

- - - - - - - - - - - - - - - -

Baptism in the New Testament always followed a person's conversion and never preceded it.

- - - - - - - - - - - - - - - -

Baptists insist that baptism is only for believers and only by immersion. The Bible teaches that baptism is a symbol of salvation in Christ: "We were therefore buried with him through baptism into death in order that, just as Christ was raised from the dead through the glory of the Father, we too may live a new life" (Romans 6:4). Baptism symbolizes the life, death, burial, and resurrection of Christ; likewise, it also signifies that a person being baptized has died to an old way of life and come alive to a new way through faith in Christ. Salvation is best pictured by the immersion of a person in water and being raised up out of the water; this was the practice in New Testament times. Thus, a person performing a baptism often says as the person is lowered into the water, "Buried with Christ in baptism," and as the person is being raised out of the water, says, "and raised to walk in newness of life."

Salvation is best pictured by the immersion of a person in water and being raised up out of the water; this was the practice in New Testament times.

Although baptism is not essential for salvation, it is nonetheless very important. It is a beautiful means of testifying that we have trusted in Jesus as our Lord and Savior; we are committed to following his example because he was baptized; and we are obeying his teachings. Furthermore, baptism is a means of declaring that Jesus is Lord since he commanded that we be baptized (Matthew 28:19). This is why the person performing a baptism often says, "In obedience to the command of the Lord Jesus Christ I baptize you in the name of the Father, the Son, and the Holy Spirit."

A Regenerate Church Membership

Baptists declare that the Bible teaches that *only persons who have been saved* are to be members of a church, and that a *person who is saved* ought to be a member of a church. For example, the Book of Acts records the establishment of the first church, which was formed after Jesus' death, resurrection, and ascension. The biblical account indicates that "the Lord added to their number daily those who were being saved" (Acts 2:47).

Baptists use various terms to describe membership in a church, such as believer's church, regenerate church, gathered church, voluntary church, born-again church, and fellowship of the redeemed. However, the basic meaning is the same: A church is a fellowship of persons who have voluntarily followed Jesus as Lord and voluntarily associated with one another under his Lordship and the guidance of the Holy Spirit. Furthermore, since Jesus commanded his disciples to be baptized, a church is to be comprised of baptized believers.

When a person seeks membership in a Baptist church, an effort is normally made to see that the person has indeed been saved. When persons who have never been a member of a church seek membership, they are asked to publicly declare their faith in Christ and to be baptized in obedience to the command of Christ. When a person seeking membership has been a member of another church, a Baptist church will accept that person into membership in various ways. However, a common denominator is determining whether the person has indeed personally placed his or her faith in Christ as Savior and Lord and been baptized as a symbol of having been saved, not as a requirement for salvation.

Congregational Church Governance

Polity is the way an organization, such as a church, functions in such matters as determining budgets, leadership, and facilities. Baptist polity places this responsibility in the hands of the entire congregation, that is, with all of the members, not just one individual or a particular group within the church. This practice is based on the examples in the Bible of congregational governance, but it is also based on other Bible-based Baptist beliefs, such as the Lordship of Christ, soul competency, and the priesthood of all believers.

Baptist polity places this responsibility in the hands of the entire congregation, that is, with all of the members, not just one individual or a particular group within the church.

"Every form of polity other than democracy somewhere infringes upon the Lordship of Christ," declared E. Y. Mullins (1860-1928), a Baptist pastor and theologian. Christ is Lord, or Head, of the church. Each member of the church is a believer priest with equal access to God through Christ and has a responsibility to seek and follow the will of God. No believer priest is superior to another. Therefore, a church is to be governed by the members, each one having an equal say or vote. Of course, the members can choose to delegate certain decisions to members or small groups in the congregation, but the ultimate responsibility for governance rests with the entire congregation.

Freedom and Variety Along with Certain Common Characteristics

The Baptist denomination does not dictate to a church its organization, form of worship, or leadership. Therefore, Baptist churches differ in these matters. However, Baptists believe that certain matters should characterize a church for it to be considered a Baptist church. Baptists believe that these matters are essential because the Bible indicates that these were features of the early churches mentioned in the New Testament, and those churches are the pattern for Baptist churches.

For example, Baptist churches have two ordinances: baptism and the Lord's Supper. Each of these is important, but neither is essential for salvation. Both are considered symbolic. The immersion of a person in water during baptism does not "wash away sin" but is a symbol that sin has been forgiven. The Lord's Supper does not consist of the literal body and blood of the Lord Jesus Christ but is symbolic of his broken body and the blood he shed for our sins.

— — — — — — — — — — — — — — — — —

Baptist churches have two ordinances: baptism and the Lord's Supper.

— — — — — — — — — — — — — — — — —

The Autonomy of Churches

The word *autonomous* means self-governing or self-directing. Thus, the autonomy of churches means that each Baptist church is independent of any outside human authority or control. In the Baptist denomination there is no person or group outside of a church that can control a church. Free from outside interference, each church selects its own pastoral leadership, determines its own budget, and provides and owns its own facilities. When Baptists form organizations other than local congregations of believers, they emphasize that none of these has any authority over a church.

Voluntary Cooperation Among Baptist Entities

Because Baptists hold fiercely to the autonomy of each congregation, they were hesitant for many years to form any organization that might threaten that independence. They came to realize, however, that through voluntary cooperation among churches and other entities, all Baptists would benefit through their combined effectiveness in evangelism, missions, ministry, and education. Baptists came to understand that churches could do more together in voluntary cooperation than an individual church could do in isolation.

Baptists came to understand that churches could do more together in voluntary cooperation than an individual church could do in isolation.

The concept of voluntary cooperation led Baptists to form various organizations to assist in carrying out the mission of Christ. These entities differ in size, organization, purpose, and names. They include associations of churches, conventions, fellowships, societies, networks, and unions. Baptists also organized institutions such as schools, medical centers, and entities for the care of children and the elderly. All of these have in common that none can exercise any control or authority over a local congregation of baptized believers.

Evangelism, Missions, Ministry, Social Action, and Christian Education—Hallmarks of Baptist Churches and Organizations

Evangelism, missions, and education are means by which Baptists help to carry out The Great Commission of the Lord Jesus Christ (Matt. 28:18-20). Ministry and social action are ways in which Baptists help to obey The Great Commandment of Jesus (Matt. 22:36-40). Voluntary cooperation enables Baptists to expand greatly their efforts in these areas.

By cooperating with other churches through various organizations Baptist churches can be part of efforts that otherwise would be beyond their capability. For example, thousands of Baptist missionaries serve throughout the world; a single church would never be able to accomplish this. Through cooperation, Baptists have established outstanding universities; this too would have been impossible for a single church to do alone.

Through cooperation, Baptists have established outstanding universities; this too would have been impossible for a single church to do alone.

Religious Freedom

Baptists cherish religious freedom, and they have put this belief into action by helping to make possible such freedom for all persons, not just for themselves. The Baptist devotion to religious freedom is closely related to all the biblical truths that comprise basic Baptist beliefs and practices. The concept of religious freedom itself rests solidly on biblical teaching and example. A free church in a free state is ideal. Neither governmental nor religious organizations ought to control religious beliefs and practices. The friendly separation of church and state makes possible religious liberty and lack of coercion in religious matters. Religious freedom, which Baptists have helped to bring about in many places in the world, enhances Baptist efforts to carry out their beliefs, polity, and practices to the benefit of Baptists and others.

Neither governmental nor religious organizations ought to control religious beliefs and practices.

Many people seem to believe that religious freedom has always existed. It has not. For centuries, most people were not free to worship, or *not* to worship, according to the dictate of their conscience. Numerous historians, Baptist and non-Baptist alike, credit Baptists with leading the way in the struggle for religious freedom.

In summary, Baptists treasure many doctrines and polities that other denominations treasure. No single doctrine or practice makes a Baptist distinctly a Baptist. However, a combination of all of the basic beliefs and practices Baptists hold dear sets Baptists apart as a distinct denomination. Through the centuries, Baptists have suffered severe persecution from both governmental and religious authorities for holding these beliefs, but they have never given them up. The Baptists' faithfulness to their convictions has enabled them to grow from a tiny persecuted band of believers to a multi-million-member denomination that ministers throughout the world.

Note: This chapter provides a brief summary of Baptist beliefs and practices. For further information, please consult the website www.baptistdistinctives.org. The website contains information on Baptist beliefs and practices, and it provides information on how to order the *Baptist Identity Series*. Another helpful source is the book *Beliefs Important to Baptists,* second edition (Dallas, Texas: BaptistWay Press, 2011).

CHAPTER 5

How Do We Relate to Other Baptists and Other Christian Groups?

By Bernard M. Spooner

Building relationships with other Christians is important for new believers and new church members. We relate to others in a variety of ways.

Relating to Others in the Congregation/Church

Belonging to a Local Congregation

We relate to each other by belonging to a local congregation and regularly attending weekly worship services and smaller Bible Study groups. One of your first priorities as a new member or new believer is to find ways *to know you belong.* This includes attending your church's worship services, being involved in a small Bible study group, and fellowshipping with other believers.

- *Attending your church's worship services* should be an ongoing part of your life to inspire and encourage you in your faith and to increase your understanding of what it means to be a Baptist Christian.
- Equally important is *becoming a regular part of a small group within your local congregation, such as a Sunday School class.* The small group should allow you to grow in your faith, make friends, and provide support for you now and in the future. For example, as part of a Sunday School class, you will pray and study the Bible regularly with others of similar age or life experience, such as children, teens, young marrieds, adult singles, and adults and seniors. Through prayer time, you can make others aware of your needs, and they can make you aware of theirs so that you can pray for one another. By studying the Bible each week, you will learn more about how to grow as a Christian. In addition, you will be able to ask questions and discuss concerns with your teacher and other individuals in the group. Also, you will be able to contact your leader or others in the group when you have a question or need help.
- It is important to *fellowship with other believers and to make friends* that will support your walk with the Lord as you navigate the ups and downs of life. This is why being part of a smaller group is so vital and important.

One of your first priorities as a new member or new believer is to find ways to know you belong.

So, *we relate to one another as Baptist Christians by becoming a part of a Sunday School class or a small group.*

Serving and Contributing

We also relate to one another by serving and contributing our time and energy within our church. There are many ways to serve. You can begin by offering to help your Bible Study teacher. For example, you could offer to make phone calls, arrange the classroom, or distribute materials. You can also help others in your small group with specific needs. As an example, if someone in your group is ill, or has lost a loved one, you can look for ways to help such as taking food to them or making an encouraging phone call. *Caution: If you express your willingness to help in some way, and you are not asked to help, don't let this hurt your feelings. Other opportunities will come, and other tasks may be more suited to your skills and abilities.*

The Bible tells us that *God has given each of us abilities and gifts for serving him.* By serving with others and using our gifts, we strengthen each other, our small group, and our church. Because we each have different gifts, we enjoy serving God and others in different ways. For example, if you are sensitive to others' needs, you may use your gift to encourage. If you are gifted in music, you may lead music in your group or sing in a church music group. If you have a gift for hospitality, you can help others socialize and have fun together. You may have special compassion for persons in need and can lead your class to meet specific needs such as for food, clothing, or other necessities. Jesus asked his disciples to tell others about him; you can do this while serving others. All of us can participate by serving on committees and in business meetings as our congregation makes decisions.

— — — — — — — — — — — — — — — —

Because we each have different gifts, we enjoy serving God and others in different ways.

— — — — — — — — — — — — — — — —

So, *we relate to others by serving and by contributing our time and energy within our church.*

Participating in Ministry and Missions

We relate to one another in our church by participating in ministry and missions. Another way to know that you belong is to take part in ministry or missions activities with other believers. Through ministry, you can help meet others' needs while indirectly being a witness for Christ. Similarly, through participation in a missions activity or event, you can help meet the needs of others while intentionally sharing Christ. Ministry or missions can occur in your local community or beyond.

In the process of participating in ministry and missions activities, you will strengthen your relationships with others and learn to reflect Jesus Christ through your efforts. Jesus said, "Whatever you did for one of the least of these brothers of mine, you did for me" (Matthew 25:40). Most likely, your church already ministers to needs within your church, your community, and beyond. For example, some families may need food or clothing. Others may be new to the country and need help learning the language and culture. There may be children who need tutoring in math or English. You can find many ways to participate with fellow church members in ministry and missions.

So *we relate to others by participating with other church members in missions and ministry.*

Your first priority for relating to other Baptist Christians is to become actively involved in your local church. By doing this you will find ways to contribute, and opportunities will open to you. As you learn and serve and make life friends, you will grow in your influence and gain confidence for your life in Christ. You will make a difference, not only for your congregation, but also for others in your life.

— — — — — — — — — — — — — — — —

Your first priority for relating to other Baptist Christians is to become actively involved in your local church.

— — — — — — — — — — — — — — — —

Relating to Other Baptists Outside the Congregation/Church

Cooperating with Other Churches in Our Denomination

We relate to other Baptist Christians by cooperating with other churches in our denomination. Most Baptist churches cooperate with a local association of churches, a convention of churches in the state or region, and a national convention, union, or fellowship of churches. Baptists believe they are directly responsible to the Lord Jesus Christ; as such, they do not operate under the authority of other churches or denominational groups. That is, each Baptist church operates as an autonomous body and is responsible for selecting its pastor and other church leaders, for developing its programs and other ministries, and for developing its operating budget, which is supported through church member tithes (10 percent of our income) and offerings. Even as autonomous bodies, most Baptist churches voluntarily cooperate with other churches through a local association, state convention, and national convention by giving to missions, praying for missions, and serving as needed to support the ministry efforts of one or more denominational groups.

Most Baptist churches cooperate with a local association of churches, a convention of churches in the state or region, and a national convention, union, or fellowship of churches.

One of the ways Baptist churches relate to other denominational bodies, such as associations and conventions, is by sending *messengers* to serve on decision-making bodies. Messengers are expected to seek guidance from God and to vote according to their own convictions in each decision. Most Baptist groups beyond the local church have committees, boards, and similar groups, and individual Baptists have the opportunity to serve on these.

The following are some avenues for serving as church members become seasoned in their Christian walk and are ready for such service:

- *Local association.* Typically, the denominational group closest to the church is the local Baptist association. Churches network through associations, which are often formed within counties or groups of counties within a local geographic area. Churches in the area join the association and provide funds for the association's work. The association helps member churches accomplish things the local church likely cannot do alone.

- *What does a local association do?* A local association serves as a resource for local churches in a variety of ways. An association may assist in starting new churches and in training Sunday School workers, missions leaders, and other leaders. Sometimes a local association may provide funds for a nearby university Baptist student ministry. Some associations establish and support a camp that is used for children, youth, and adult church events. Churches support local association ministries and missions by providing financial resources and volunteer leaders to serve in these ministries.

- *State convention or fellowship.* Beyond the local Baptist association is the state convention or fellowship. In parts of the country with many Baptist churches, churches have formed state or multi-state conventions. When there are only a few churches, a fellowship is formed. Whereas fellowships are usually dependent on outside missions funding, state conventions are typically able to support themselves. As more churches are started and as churches are able to provide more money, a fellowship becomes a convention. In some instances, a fellowship is made up of churches from more than one state.

- *What does a state convention do?* Like local associations, the state convention helps churches collectively carry out and support ministries that a local church would never be able to do alone. For example, most state conventions partner with churches and associations to start new congregations. Many state conventions establish and support children's homes, retirement homes, and hospitals. In states where Baptists have a long history, state conventions support Baptist colleges and universities and provide graduate degree scholarships for pastors and others called to church vocational ministry. Many states provide vocational student ministry leaders for Baptist, state, and private college and university campuses. State conventions provide personnel to train and support churches in various ministries such as Sunday School, missions education, building consultation, disaster relief, and advocacy work for poor and minority groups. Also, state conventions assist churches by receiving and distributing mission funds from churches.

- *National conventions, unions, and fellowships.* At the broadest level, churches relate to other Baptists through national conventions, unions, and fellowships. These groups usually are started for specific purposes and assist churches in accomplishing tasks a church may not be able to do alone. For example, they may commission and financially support missionaries or provide education for ministers. As mentioned above, no group, including national conventions, has authority over the churches they serve because local Baptist churches operate as autonomous bodies. One leader stated, "The Baptist denomination, of course, has no prescribed 'rules' for how these organizations are formed or what titles are used for them. Furthermore, often more than one 'nationwide' organization exists within a nation or country."

- *What does a national convention, union, or fellowship do?* A national convention, union, or fellowship facilitates collective efforts related to missions and ministries within a nation and to other nations. The various states, provinces, or other regions within a nation voluntarily cooperate to start churches or to meet other needs.

Some regions have strong Baptist churches and influences while other areas may have few churches. So, the national convention, union, or fellowship seeks to expand the impact of Christ in these states, provinces, or regions of a nation.

- Baptists have a history of sending missionaries to parts of the world where the message of Christ is needed. For many years, Baptists sent missionaries to other nations, but now Baptists in these nations have conventions of strong churches. These conventions or unions are now sending out international missionaries. Sometimes national groups address moral issues and social concerns such as poverty, child labor, and religious liberty. Church contributions make national and international missions possible. Baptists have a strong history of cooperating and supporting missions.

- *Other types of groups:* Other Baptist groups organize around common interests. Examples of such groups are the Baptist Joint Committee for Religious Liberty, the Baptist History and Heritage Society, and groups related to colleges and universities.

How can you be involved in the association, state convention, or a national convention, union, or fellowship? Just as a local church has ministries and committees where persons are needed to do the work, the association and each of the conventions or unions also has committees, boards, commissions, and ministries where important work or decisions need to be made. As you grow and learn and serve in your church, you may volunteer to be involved in your association or another group.

No group, including national conventions, has authority over the churches they serve because local Baptist churches operate as autonomous bodies.

So, *we relate to other Baptists by cooperating with other churches in our denomination.*

Relating to Baptists Internationally

Baptists Relate to Other Baptists Worldwide Through the Baptist World Alliance

The Baptist World Alliance (BWA), formed in London, England, in 1905, is a worldwide coalition of Baptist churches and organizations. In 2012, BWA was comprised of 223 groups representing 120 countries and more than 42 million baptized believers in 177,000 churches. The goals of the BWA are to unite Baptists worldwide, to lead in world evangelism, to respond to people in need, and to defend human rights. The alliance has six regional or geographical fellowships:

- North American Baptist Fellowship
- Asia Pacific Baptist Fellowship (formerly Asian Baptist Federation)
- All-African Baptist Fellowship
- Caribbean Baptist Fellowship
- Union of Baptists in South America
- European Baptist Federation

A Baptist World Congress is held every five years, and usually moves to a different continent each time it meets. In 2005, the Congress was held in Birmingham, England, to celebrate the 100th anniversary of BWA. In addition to BWA Congresses, the BWA Executive Committee meets every year in different areas of the world.

The BWA is supported by individuals, churches, and various conventions, unions, and fellowships from all over the world. Many churches include the BWA in their church budgets. In addition to the regular budget, the Baptist World Aid arm of the BWA relies on monetary gifts from Baptists so that it can respond to disasters around the world, provide food and other needs during severe droughts, and help displaced persons who seek shelter and safety from political conflict. Providing water wells is one of the most significant programs of Baptist World Aid as it meets the critical need for fresh water.

_____ __ __ __ __ __ __ __ __ __ __ __ __ __ __ __

Many churches include the BWA in their church budgets.

_____ __ __ __ __ __ __ __ __ __ __ __ __ __ __ __

So, *we can relate to other Baptists worldwide through the Baptist World Alliance.*

In addition to relating to other Baptist Christians in your congregation, look for opportunities to be involved with Baptists outside of your congregation. As you become aware of what other Baptist churches and Baptist groups do, you will better understand how the message of Christ is spread beyond your community to the rest of your region, to the nation, and ultimately, to the world.

Relating to Other Christians

While Baptists have many ways to relate to other Baptists in their community and beyond, they often cooperate with other Christian churches or organizations for various causes. In most local communities, many people would suffer unmet needs without the help of Christians and others who live nearby. For example, local churches often partner with area Christian groups and churches to assist people with emergency needs such as food, clothing, and shelter. In addition, Baptist churches may work with other Christians to address a moral concern in the community or nationally. Another excellent way Baptists can relate to other Christian groups is to celebrate at Easter or Christmas through special music presentations or pageants involving persons from churches of several denominations.

Although Baptists hold beliefs that are different from other denominations, we respect persons of different Christian faith traditions. For example, Baptists baptize by immersion while others baptize by sprinkling or pouring. Likewise, various denominations may have different types of church governance or ways of finding a new pastor. Even so, we can be a source of encouragement to all, and we can receive encouragement from other Christians as we seek to share Christ with the world. Certainly, we remain faithful to our own convictions and bring glory to our Lord by extending a hand of fellowship with others who seek to honor Christ. Together we can make a greater impact in the community as we point people to Christ.

Although Baptists hold beliefs that are different from other denominations, we respect persons of different Christian faith traditions.

So, *we can relate to non-Baptist Christian groups locally by partnering with them to meet needs in the community and by celebrating special Christian holidays.*

Non-Baptist Christians are significant in their influence and impact for Christ. As a Baptist, you will do well to have a positive attitude and appreciation for Christians who are involved in different faith traditions. While they may have difference experiences in some ways, they are a part of the wider family of Christians, and they too seek to honor our Lord in their churches and ministries.

Relating to Non-Christians

Baptists need to relate to non-Christian persons as well as to Christians. Jesus intended for all believers to be witnesses for him. So, you are challenged to cultivate relationships with individuals who are not Christians and to learn how to have conversations with them.

One principle for witnessing is to be a good listener, demonstrating an interest in and care for people who do not have a personal relationship with our Lord. We can learn to be "winsome" persons who attract others to our Savior, while the Holy Spirit is the One who convicts persons of their need for the salvation that comes through Jesus Christ.

— — — — — — — — — — — — — — — —

One principle for witnessing is to be a good listener, demonstrating an interest in and care for people who do not have a personal relationship with our Lord.

— — — — — — — — — — — — — — — —

Summary

Relating to other Baptists and to non-Baptist Christians is part of the life of a Baptist Christian. You should start by becoming involved in your own congregation. As you grow in your faith, you may extend your involvement beyond your local church. In the beginning, however, your first priority is to relate to Baptists in your own church through worship and a small group such as a Sunday School group. This is important for all believers, but it is especially beneficial for new believers and new church members. You need the fellowship and encouragement that comes from developing new friends in your own church. Also, as you grow as a Christian, you will want to become more involved. Some possibilities are as follows:

- You can relate by serving along with fellow Baptists. This is an excellent way to discover your unique gifts and abilities and to learn to use them effectively.
- You can volunteer to participate in missions or ministry projects. Ministry may relate to persons in your congregation who have specific needs such as persons who need

tutoring, or elderly persons who need assistance with household tasks or transportation.

- You can learn to relate to Baptists outside of your congregation by becoming aware of the local Baptist association, the state or regional convention, and the national convention, union, or fellowship.
- You can become aware of the work of the Baptist World Alliance and consider becoming involved through prayer, financial support, or attendance at meetings when possible.
- You can seek opportunities to relate to non-Baptist persons and churches. Many believers in your community honor Christ and can benefit from encouragement in their faith and service to Christ.
- Finally, you can pray for your small group, for the ministries of your church, and the ministries and mission work of Baptists all over the world. You can also pray for other Christians who are seeking to honor our Lord while meeting the needs of others.

In the best sense, being a Baptist gives you an opportunity to grow and to become a person who makes a difference within your own congregation and in your community and beyond.

Start with your church worship and a small group Bible study such as your Sunday School class. As time goes on, pray about opportunities for further involvement and service in your church.

God places each of us in this world to influence others positively and to share Jesus Christ through all areas of our lives. May God bless every day of your life.

CHAPTER 6

Talking with Children about Faith, Baptism, and Following Christ

By Thomas L. Sanders

When a second grade boy was asked about his favorite thing at church, he answered, "Big church." When pushed to explain, he went on to say, "I like it when the pastor puts his story in the big story." This idea of the powerful influence that pastors, lay leaders, and parents have on a child is a common theme from my doctoral research and subsequent research conducted as a part of Dallas Baptist University's Master of Arts in Children's Ministry and Master of Arts in Family Ministry programs.[18]

As I conducted this research, I discovered that children have a unique relationship with their pastor, even when the pastor does not know the children's names. Sunday School leaders have a similar place in influencing a child. However, in interviews with children it has been discovered that the role of parents is very significant, because they are the first people the child wants to talk with about his or her interest in faith. The disconnect is when parents in the same set of interviews articulated that they were not equipped to have those discussions. This chapter will offer guidance for pastors, ministers, lay leaders, and parents to help them better understand how to talk to children about faith, baptism, and following Christ.

...In interviews with children it has been discovered that the role of parents is very significant because they are the first people the child wants to talk with about his or her interest in faith.

Don't Throw the Child Out with the Baptism Water

In recent years, Baptists have celebrated the 400th anniversary of their beginnings in 1609 and the subsequent publishing of *A Short Declaration of the Mistery of Iniquity* [sic] (1612) by Thomas Helwys. Hard to miss in this genesis are the central issues of religious liberty and believer's baptism in the formation of the first Baptist church by Englishmen John Smyth and Thomas Helwys in Amsterdam. While working in a Mennonite bake house in 1609, these two leaders and their followers argued that conversion and confession must precede a believer's baptism. In the years to follow, Baptists rejected the baptism of children and argued for postponing this occasion until youth or even young adulthood, using a "Baptist catechism" to ensure the converts were prepared for this experience. As a result, the Baptist Sunday School Board in 1892 published *A Catechism for Bible Teaching* by John Broadus.[19]

The rise of Sunday Schools, revivals, and Vacation Bible Schools (Everyday Bible Schools as they were known at first) came in the 1800s and early 1900s. Southern Baptists in America were baptizing children in early adolescence and late childhood. By the 1960s, the Southern Baptist Convention reported the first large number of preschool baptisms.[20] This growing trend— the number reaching over 4,000 baptisms of five-year-olds and younger—created a great deal of discussion. Leading pastors such as W. A. Criswell of First Baptist Church, Dallas, Texas developed practices that prevented children under nine years of age from being baptized because in his ministry he saw so many of them re-baptized as adolescents.[21] The question for Baptists had moved from *if* a child can become a Christian and be baptized to *when* a child can become a Christian and be baptized, to *how* they become a Christian and be baptized. In the 400 years since the formation of the Baptist denomination, the place of children related to conversion and baptism has been developing in concept and practice.

The matter of *if, when,* and *how* a child can become a Christian and be baptized is problematic for Baptists who consider themselves people of the Book. This is because the Book, or the Bible, does not contain direct guidance on this matter. When it comes to conversion and baptism, children are treated the same way as adults. However, there are Christians and Bible scholars who look to the six specific cases where Scripture records that a person and his whole house believed or were baptized, and they find that as grounds for infant baptism.[22] Their assertion is that the terms *entire house* or *household* assume that infants and children were included in those who were baptized. Baptists have rejected this assumption arguing for believer's baptism only.

Since the *if* questions seem to be settled for Baptists, the *when* questions become more critical. In a survey of literature, both current and historical, one of the best statements comes from the writer Gaines Dobbins, author of *Winning the Children* (1953). In his attempt to wrestle with the *when* at the early stages of the increase in baptisms, he wrote:

Let no mistake be made: the child must be won to Christ or the child be lost to Christ. How early? No arbitrary answer can be given. Children vary in intellectual grasp, in background, in spiritual capacity and sensitivity, in privilege and opportunity. The child needs a savior when he has consciously become a sinner. The child becomes a sinner when his wrongdoing is recognized as against God, not merely as disobedience to parents and elders.[23]

He argues not for age designation for conversion, because of the individual nature of the rate of development, intellectual capacity, type of affinity, and environment, but focuses on the understanding of sin and personal accountability to God, not adults.

In the interviews with children after they have become Christians, there is a clear struggle for them to understand sin in context of God over parents. Moral developmental theories, such as Peck-Havinhurst, Piaget, and Kohlberg all emphasize the role of parental and adult authority in avoiding punishment and making moral decisions. Dobbins' point is that children must understand that they are lost before they can be saved. In addition to understanding sin, children both in the research interviews and in the moral development theories display a desire to please adults. Parents, ministers, and leaders must be careful to assess whether the children are expressing a desire or want to please adults and receive public affirmation, or whether they are experiencing the need to be saved because of conviction.

Dobbins' point is that children must understand that they are lost before they can be saved.

In our studies, when children were asked, "Who sins?" a common answer was "bad people" or "the Devil." This kind of response should not be shocking; children developmentally place people in categories and may even shift the blame to others. For this reason, parents and leaders must seek to converse with children rather than merely present information to them or indoctrinate the right answer into the child's memory. In the dialogue of faith, understanding can grow and develop as leaders rely on the Holy Spirit and a trusting relationship with the child.

In American culture, even more today than twenty-five years ago, children have a greater sense of entitlement and influence.[24] Today's culture is not one where children have to wait for and work toward many goals, and children can feel they should get what they want when they want it. This idea can be carried over to the church and baptism. If they want to be baptized, then their parents should make it happen. In conversations with parents, statements that are often heard are, "She really wants to be baptized," or "How will we tell him that he needs to wait to be baptized?" Parents and church leaders would not have to look far in Scripture to see that parents and church leaders are given a stewardship of the child. While a child who expresses that he or she has already become a Christian should never be discouraged, parents and other leaders may want to take steps toward baptism to affirm the child's conversion. Leaders should take careful steps to orchestrate the preparation and follow-up to baptism. A part of the process can be spending time in discussion and dialogue until a point where parents and ministers feel that the child expresses an understanding of and accountability for sin. This understanding does not mean the child can express it in terms emotionally or cognitively, as do adults, but at a minimum, the child can tell his or her story of confession and conversion.

While a child who expresses that he or she has already become a Christian should never be discouraged, parents and other leaders may want to take steps toward baptism to affirm the child's conversion.

As mentioned earlier, W. A. Criswell developed a practice of not baptizing children under age nine, because of the questions and prevalence of rebaptism among adolescents who were baptized earlier than age eight. This concern is born out of other areas of research as well. In 1993, the Home Mission Board of the Southern Baptist Convention's research indicated 35.3 percent of those being baptized were re-baptized.[25] The simple fact may be that children cannot remember the experience significantly enough to overcome their new intense feelings of guilt brought on by the development of abstract thoughts and the challenges of adolescence. There is also the issue that the conversion experiences of friends in adolescence may look different and more intense than these now-adolescent students can remember about their own experience. This issue may not be the validity of the conversion and baptism, but the failure to make the experience memorable enough in the years to come.

Joining Them on the Journey

At times, in education and philosophy, children have been seen as blank sheets of wax on which experience and people can make fresh and lasting impressions. Currently, there is a greater understanding that children are born with certain personality traits and temperaments that can be shaped and influenced to some degree based on good or poor environments. Sofia Cavalletti, in *The Religious Potential of the Child* (1983), and David Hay and Rebecca Nye, in *The Spirit of the Child* (2006), stipulate that all children begin a search for God, and when they do not make that connection, they connect with something less meaningful than a relationship with the Creator.[26] Parents from the beginning have a role in creating an environment where the young child can more easily connect with God, Jesus, and the Bible. When children are active in church and their parents talk about faith at home, children will naturally begin to ask questions. This instance is especially true with younger siblings. The first child has only adults to talk with, but younger siblings benefit from, as Albert Bandura (1977) describes, *vicarious learning.*[27] They observe, they listen, and they learn not only how to speak the language, but also how to navigate the situation based on those observations.

When children are active in church and their parents talk about faith at home, children will naturally begin to ask questions.

A common occurrence in a faith-rich family is for a child in kindergarten and first grade to begin asking questions about baptism. Seeing someone being baptized, especially the baptism of a friend or sibling, can be a powerful motivator for a child.

This motivation is not bad, but it can be misguided. The first step in the conversation can begin with these types of experiences, but interest is not necessarily a sign of conviction. In this vein, parents should be careful of these motivation factors by avoiding praying with children that they become Christians at the earliest possible date. This is a great prayer for a mother and father to pray together, but when prayed in the presence of the child, it can become a strong motivator instead of relying on the work of the Holy Spirit. Also, when events transpire in families, such as the death of a relative, parents should be careful of saying that if the child becomes a Christian, he or she can see the deceased person in heaven one day. In this instance, the deceased relative becomes the reason instead of a relationship with Jesus Christ. Finally, children can be influenced by rewards both tangible and intangible. A Sunday School class setting would not be the best place to have a party for a child who has been baptized, especially when other children may not have had this experience. The experience of being left out is a strong motivator for children.

Parents should be careful of these motivation factors by avoiding praying with children that they become Christians at the earliest possible date. This is a great prayer for a mother and father to pray together, but when prayed in the presence of their children, it can become a strong motivator instead of relying on the work of the Holy Spirit.

Parents, teachers, and leaders should be careful to construct language *with* children, not *for* children. As parents and leaders listen more and ask questions, they can begin to construct meaning with children and eliminate misconceptions on both the adult and child side of the conversation. In interviews with young ones, these influential adults often use the language of faith correctly, but when asked to explain the meaning, they are at a loss. Questions and follow-up questions should be asked in a way that allows the child to explain concepts, like sin. A child who responds that sin is doing "bad things" might be challenged to think of sin in the context of choosing to do things "our way" instead of God's way. In this discussion, children will be encouraged to move beyond the bad things to think more in the context of obeying God. When children use the titles for God like Lord and Savior, these terms should not be glossed over by the adult when talking with the child. The adult may ask the child what the word means and then explain, "Savior means that Jesus died to take the penalty for our sin." In understanding those words, one of the most difficult questions for children to answer is "Why did Jesus die?" The most common answer is "to save us from our sins." However, when asked what this means, children rarely have an answer. It is as if they have memorized the phrase, but there is little understanding beyond this statement.

The biggest trap for parents and ministry leaders who talk with children is to default to using questions that can be answered with a simple yes or no. Children naturally want to please adults and especially adults who represent God. It is essential not to overdo verbal or physical signs of affirmation when a child gives a correct answer. Research today is showing that children as young as toddlers are able to read emotions and thoughts of adults and modify their responses accordingly. Sometimes, a simple "thank you" is enough affirmation. Also, remember that children need time to think and consider their answers. Encourage the child from the onset of the conversation that it is okay to take time to answer questions, and that the conversation is not a test. Another technique is to say to the child that if he or she does not understand something, he or she can feel free to ask you to say it another way. The words and phrases that a leader might use may be different from those the child hears in the home environment. This gives the child another way to understand the question.

The biggest trap for parents and ministry leaders who talk with children is to default to using questions that can be answered with a simple yes or no.

Be careful about using abstract color-coded tracts that represent theological concepts. For younger children, this layer of symbols can be more confusing and distracting than the actual concepts. In addition, these tools rarely encourage discussion, but rather offer a presentation that calls for a yes answer instead of furthering understanding. One additional word of caution: Using a color such as black to represent sin can really send the wrong message to children who have darker skin and can seem culturally insensitive to parents and community leaders.

Finally, the Bible is the best tool to use with children. Parents and ministers can use the following verses to discuss conversion and baptism with children:

- God loves you and has a great plan for you. (Psalm 139:13-16)
- We have all sinned. (Romans 3:23)
- Even though we choose to sin, God still loves us and offers to forgive us. (Romans 5:8)
- Jesus died for us. (John 3:16)
- You become a Christian by saying that Jesus is your Savior and Lord. (Romans 10:9)

A good resource for continuing the discussion with any child who has questions is *When Can I?* (2001), written by Thomas Sanders.

Parent Involvement and Ministry Support

For a variety of reasons, churches have often taken the lead in sharing the gospel with children. Parents at times feel unequipped to have that discussion. Church leaders should begin early and often to help parents become comfortable with this role and process. Providing seminars, podcasts, and other events to train parents is essential. Doing this is not to encourage parents to push their children, but to be better guides for their sons and daughters. Guide parents to become comfortable with sharing their own faith stories. Children need to hear how their parents experienced conversion and how their relationship with Jesus influences their daily lives. Parents should encourage their ministry leaders to provide this type of help early and often.

When a child indicates in a church setting that he or she wants to become a Christian, leaders should seek to involve parents in the discussion if at all possible, especially when the child comes from a Christian home. Be careful not to rob parents of the opportunity to be a part of their child's conversion experience. Not only should parents be involved in this experience, but also in follow-up discipleship that prepares the child for baptism. Fathers and mothers can make their desires known to ministers and children's ministry leaders. Discipleship after conversion and before/after baptism should take place in the home and in the church. If children do not have parents who are Christians, Sunday School leaders or church leaders should take the time to provide personal discipleship. These experiences could include:

- Working through discipleship resources such as *I Am a Christian Now* (LifeWay Press)
- Making a memory box or book that contains copies of worship services, VBS, or other promotional material that will help the child remember this important time
- Writing and recording the child's story of how he or she became a Christian
- Keeping letters written to the child by family members and others related to their conversion and baptism
- Taking photos of the child and the minister who baptized the child
- Keeping the child's first Lord's Supper cup

Talking with Children About Baptism and the Lord's Supper

Parents, pastors, and leaders should keep in mind each year when children enter worship for the first time that these are key opportunities to introduce the doctrines of baptism and the Lord's Supper. Baptism is one of the most powerful symbols of our faith and marks inclusion into the church, but even among Baptists it symbolizes different meanings, including these:

- Symbolic of internal change brought about by personal faith in Jesus Christ
- Symbolic identification with the death, burial, and resurrection of Christ
- Symbolic cleansing of sin
- Entry into the church
- Obedience to Christ's command[28]

For the children in our research, the overwhelming meaning of baptism was not the symbolic washing way of sin, but the literal. For a variety of reasons, many children expressed that their conversion was not complete without the washing with water. In attempts to interpret this finding, several explanations arose. The first was that in baptismal services and conversations around these occurrences, parents and others neglect to tell the stories of how a person becomes a Christians. Instead, the focus is on "She came forward to be baptized." A conscious effort should be made to tell the story that led to the day of their baptism.

The second reason may be harder to counter. Baptism is a very concrete, sensational, and experiential event for the participant and the observers. The power of this experience or the expectation of the experience may actually overpower simple words of explanation. Piaget describes this as centration. Parents and leaders may have to continue the process of clarification for the child. The beginning point is to speak of baptism in conjunction with conversion. A simple explanation is showing that you have accepted Jesus as your Savior and that in his death, burial, and resurrection, Jesus took the punishment for your sin.

— — — — — — — — — — — — — — —

The beginning point is to speak of baptism in conjunction with conversion.

— — — — — — — — — — — — — — —

Children may have friends who are a part of Christian denominations that practice infant baptism. As a part of preparation for baptism, church leaders and parents should consider discussion with children about why Baptists do not practice infant baptism. One option is to tell the story of the Baptists' beginnings. The following is a brief story to share with children:

> In 1608, a group of Christians gathered secretly in Lincolnshire, England. They wanted to worship and read the Bible in a way different from what was legal in England. King James I and the government tried to put these people in jail for their beliefs. They left England and went to Holland, where they could practice their faith. In this group were two men named John Smyth and Thomas Helwys. These men began to read the Bible and decided that baptizing an infant was not in the Bible and that a person must accept Jesus as their Savior before being baptized. Smyth and Helwys did not believe that parents should have their babies baptized because the young children did not understand what they were doing. Smyth baptized himself and baptized everyone in the small group.
>
> In 1612, Thomas Helwys believed that God wanted this group of baptized believers to go back to England and start the first Baptist church in a place called Spitalfields outside London. Thomas Helwys decided to write a book about his beliefs on baptism and that people should be free to worship God in their own way. He sent the book to King James I. King James I put Thomas Helwys in jail, and he was never set free. He died in jail for his beliefs.
>
> When a person is being baptized today, we must remember the Baptists like Thomas Helwys. He was willing to stand up for his beliefs in baptism and the freedom to worship God in his own way.[29]

Being excluded from something important can be a powerful motivator, and so parents and ministers should consider the youngest congregants in observing the Lord's Supper. Before the child sees the Lord's Supper for the first time, parents should take time to discuss it with their child. Historically, Baptist churches have believed that a person must have accepted Christ as Savior, and in some cases been baptized, before participating in the Lord's Supper. Church leaders should educate parents on what the church's practices are in this area. Also, church leaders must see to the education of children. One idea is that once a year when observing the Lord's Supper, invite one child or several children to come forward and ask (pre-planned) questions. The minister can guide the discussion, teaching the entire congregation in the process. The Lord's Supper can also be a useful tool to teach children between their conversion experience and their baptism. Children who are not participating can be encouraged to draw pictures of all the ways Jesus showed His love for people. Parents can explain that waiting to take the Lord's Supper will make it more meaningful.

Being excluded from something important can be a powerful motivator, and so parents and ministers should consider the youngest congregants in observing the Lord's Supper.

Conclusion

The irony of talking to children about following Christ is that children may have more to teach adults than we have to teach them. When Jesus was asked, "Who is the greatest in the kingdom of heaven?" (Matthew 18:1), Jesus did not place a pastor, parent, theologian, or CEO in their midst. He selected a child and issued the challenge to his twelve disciples that they must become like a child. Many interpretations can be made of this selection, but the clear message in this verse and those that follow in the same chapter is that children were of prime importance to the Son of God and that guiding them in the way of faith should not be taken lightly so as to make them stumble. Take seriously the challenge to join children on the journey to know, trust, love, follow, and serve Christ.

Resources

Bandura, Albert. *Social Learning Theory*. Englewood Cliffs, N.J.: Prentice Hall, 1977.

Capps, T., and S. Shaw. *I'm a Christian Now: Older Child*. Nashville, TN: Lifeway Press, 2003.

Cavalletti, Sofia. *The Religious Potential of the Child*. New York: Paulist Press, 1983.

Clarke, Jean I., Bredehoft, David, & Connie Dawson. *How Much Is Enough?* New York: Marlowe & Company, 2004.

Coble, William B. "Problems Related to New Testament Teachings." Edited by Clifford Ingle. *Children and Conversion*. Nashville, TN: Broadman Press, 1970.

Criswell, W. A. "Criswell says child should be junior age before baptized." *Baptist Standard* 81, no. 21 (1969): 4.

Dobbins, Gaines S. *Winning the Children*. Nashville: Broadman Press, 1953.

Garrett, J. L., Jr. "The Theology and Practice of Baptism: A Southern Baptist view." *Southwestern Journal of Theology* 28, no. 2 (1986) 65-72.

Hay, David, and Rebecca Nye. *The Spirit of the Child*. London: Jessica Kingsley Publishers, 2006.

Ingle, Clifford. *Children and Conversion*. Nashville: Broadman Press, 1970.

Leonard, B. J. *Once Saved, Almost Saved: Revisiting Baptists and Conversion*. Paper presented at Parchman Lecture II at Baylor University, Waco, TX, 2008.

McBeth, Leon. *The Baptist Heritage*. Nashville, Tenn: Broadman Press, 1987.

Sanders, Thomas. *When Can I?* Nashville, TN: Broadman & Holman, 2001.

Sanders, Thomas. "The Kingdom of God Belongs to Such as These: Exploring the Conversion Experiences of Baptist Children." Doctoral dissertation, Dallas Baptist University, 2009.

Wingfield, M. "60 percent of baptisms are rebaptisms." *Western Recorder* 169 (1995): 14.

APPENDIX

Teaching Plans

Teaching Plan for Chapter 1
What Does Having Personal Faith Mean, and How Does That Affect My Daily Life?

Teaching Aim: To lead members to identify the primary aspects of faith, and to determine whether these are being manifested in their lives.

Introduction

Write the following questions on the board, or make copies for distribution to the class:

1. What is faith?
2. How is faith different from belief?
3. Who is the object of Christian faith?
4. How is faith received?
5. What is justification?
6. Why is baptism so important?
7. What is sanctification?
8. In what ways is sanctification manifested in a Christian's life?

Challenge class members to discover answers to these questions during this study and to determine how each of these is having an impact on their lives.

Chapter Study

Ask members to share examples of a demonstration of faith they have heard such as sitting in a chair. You may want to share the example given by the author at the beginning of this chapter. Then ask members what these examples have in common. (Faith was demonstrated by an action taken.)

Write this definition of faith on the board: *Faith is the mental and emotional capacity to trust or have confidence in something or someone.* Share background information from the first section in this chapter that supports and explains this statement.

Ask members to share examples of the different objects in which a person can place faith. Then ask, *Who and what is the object of New Testament faith?* Be prepared to present the information from this section of chapter one as their various suggestions are discussed. Close this time of discussion with the statement, *Jesus – his life, death, burial and resurrection – is the object of Christian faith.*

Share the following statement – *No one can come to God unless God's Spirit draws him or urges him to come* – and then ask the class members why they agree or disagree with it. Share information from this section of chapter one before concluding with these two statements: (1) *For the believer, faith is a gift from God.* (2) *The Holy Spirit is the agent who brings God's gift of faith to the believer.*

Then lead in a time of discussion based on the next section of this chapter as you guide members to discover answers to the following three questions:

1. What is justification?
2. What is sanctification?
3. What is the significance of baptism?

Ask members to share examples of how sanctification is manifested in a Christian's life. Be prepared to include the suggested manifestations mentioned by the author. These are referred to as spiritual disciplines and include public worship, Bible study, prayer, tithing, witnessing, and ministry.

Application

Lead members through a summary of each of the questions shared at the beginning of this study. Ask them to determine their personal responses to the following questions:

1. Do I understand what it means to have faith in someone or something?
2. When did I first believe in the gospel teachings?

3. When did I first ask Jesus to save me from sin and become the Lord of my life?
4. Do I recall when the Holy Spirit convicted me of sin and came into my heart?
5. Do I feel fully forgiven by God?
6. Have I forgiven myself of sins I've committed in the past?
7. Have I been baptized as a testimony of my salvation?
8. Have I received the gift of sanctification?
9. Am I living according to acting on that gift?

Close with prayer for continued reflection and response to each of these questions.

Teaching Plan for Chapter 2
Why Is Belonging to a Local Church Important?

Teaching Aim: To lead members to determine their response to the following question: *Why am I a member of this church?*

Introduction

Share the following case study: *Mary and her family used to attend church on a regular basis, but recently they have allowed other pursuits to gradually cause them to lose interest in church. It began with children's Sunday soccer games and gymnastic activities and shifted to other kinds of recreational pursuits for all members of the family. Occasionally one of their former church friends asks about their absence, and the response is usually, "We just got to where we felt that participation in a church wasn't all that important. We are now doing 'home church.'"*

Ask members to share some of the things they could say to Mary and her husband about the importance of church. List these ideas on the board. Then ask class members to recall times when they might have had a tendency to agree with Mary. This chapter will help us to be better prepared to respond to the question, *Why am I a member of this church?*

Chapter Study

Begin by writing these questions on the board, or make copies for distribution:

1. What is a church? (See the information in the sections "Not a Building — People"; "*Ecclesia* — the Called Out"; and "A Fellowship of Believers.")

2. What is the church's mission? (See the section, "The Mission of the Church.")

3. What should the church do? (See the section, "What Are the Essential Things a Church Must Do?")

4. Why do I need to be active in a church? (See the section, "How Does My Faith Relate to My Church and to Its Mission?")

5. What is my role in the church? (See the section, "Do I Really Have Gifts for Serving God?")

Then divide the class into five groups. Assign one question to each group and ask them to find answers to their question in the assigned sections from chapter two. Allow ten minutes for this activity before reassembling the class. Ask each group to report on the answers to their assigned question. Answers should include the following:

1. *Question one.* The purpose of the church is to be a fellowship of persons who have received Christ and who are living the way of Christ, through his grace and their faith, to work obediently with him to bring others to God. The church is an *ecclesia*, which means *the called-out ones.*

2. *Question two.* The mission of a church, which is composed of baptized believers who share a personal commitment to Jesus Christ as Savior and Lord, is to be a redemptive body in Christ, through the power of the Holy Spirit growing toward Christian maturity through worship, proclamation and witness, nurture and education, and ministry to the whole world that God's purpose may be achieved. Read Matthew 16:18-19; 28:19-20; Acts 1:8; 2 Corinthians 5:18; and Ephesians 3:8-11.

3. *Question three.* Worship, proclamation and witness, nurture and education, and ministry are all essential. They relate directly to one another.

4. *Question four.* Christ established the church and died for the church. Our justification and sanctification are tied to the church. The church is Christ in the world. The church is God's plan for involving his people in bringing about his kingdom in the hearts of people everywhere.

5. *Question five.* We have been called and gifted to minister. When Christ called us to be his followers, he gave each of us a ministry to perform and equipped us to perform that ministry. Many different ministries and gifts are needed in the church. Some gifts are for use in the church and some in the world. The church needs to affirm the callings and gifts of believers.

Application

Ask members to respond to the question, *Why am I a member of this church?* You may want to have each person share his or her response in groups of two. Close with prayer for your church and for a renewed commitment to become a more effective church member.

Teaching Plan for Chapter 3
Who Are the Baptists, and How Are We Contributing to the Cause of Christ?

Teaching Aim: To present a lecture on this chapter and lead members to complete a study guide based on this presentation

Introduction

Begin by reading the first paragraph of this chapter. Share with the class that the purpose of this study is to discover how Baptists began and what their contribution has been to the cause of Christ. Distribute the study guides and ask members to use these to record information shared during this study. Following is the study guide with suggested answers *(italicized and in parentheses)*. Prepare the study guide for your class members by deleting these answers on their copies before printing them. Provide space on the study guide after each question for the class members to write their responses to each question.

Chapter Study

As you present a lecture based on this chapter, prompt the class members to record information in their study guides (suggested responses are in italics in parentheses; a study guide suitable for copying and handing out is available after this Teaching Plan):

A History of Baptists

1. When did the first identifiable Baptist churches emerge? *(seventeenth century).*

2. How were they different from the established church? *(Believer's baptism rather than infant baptism; voluntary church membership rather than enforced membership; authority of the Bible rather than the church; salvation through grace by faith rather than rituals and works-related salvation.)*

3. What movement was sweeping through Europe that led to the widespread challenge to the Roman Catholic Church? *(The Reformation, led by men such as Martin Luther, Ulrich Zwingli, Thomas Cranmer, and John Calvin)*

4. What early groups developed before the first English Baptists? *(Anabaptists — they held similar doctrines but practiced radical separation from the world; Puritans — desired to remove the last vestiges of Roman Catholicism from the Church of England; Separatists — advocated total separation from, rather than revision of, the Anglican church.)*

5. Who organized the first English Baptist churches? *(John Smyth and Thomas Helwys)*

6. What cardinal Baptist principles were established by the Smyth-Helwys-Murton congregation? *(Believer's baptism, religious liberty, new church starts, and enduring persecution.)*

7. What title was given to the group of Baptists referred to in question 6? *(General Baptists).*

8. What title was given to another group of Baptists in England? *(Particular Baptists).* They differed from General Baptists in the following ways:

(a) *(Maintained a relationship with the Puritans)*
(b) *(Said that Christ's atonement was limited to the "particular" or elect)*
(c) *(Engaged more directly with the surrounding culture and society)*
(d) *(Practiced baptism by immersion rather than by pouring)*

(e) *(Put more emphasis on confessions of faith)*
(f) *(Placed greater emphasis on scriptural authority)*

9. Freedom of conscience and scriptural authority are closely aligned with belief in _____ *(religious liberty)* and _____ *(separation of church and state)*.

10. Who were some of the most important contributors to the beginning of Baptist work in America? *(Roger Williams and John Clarke)*

11. What movement in the mid-eighteenth century greatly influenced the growth of Baptists in colonial life? *(Great Awakening)* Much of this growth came from what group of churches? *(Congregationalist churches)* Who were the two specific people most responsible for this growth? *(Isaac Backus, John Leland)*

12. Baptist historians regard the first church founded in North Carolina, whose name was the _____ *(Sandy Creek Baptist Church)*, as one of the mother congregations of these Baptists: _____ *(Southern Baptists)*.

13. The passion for sharing the gospel also translated into another Baptist contribution to Christianity, that of Baptists' fervent _____ *(support of missions)*.

14. The best known and perhaps most important pioneers in the modern missions movement were these two British Baptists: _____ *(Andrew Fuller)* and _____ *(William Carey)*.

15. Other Baptist pioneers in the missions movement include these leaders: _____, _____, _____, _____, _____, _____, _____, _____, and _____. *(Joshua Marshman, William Ward, Luther Rice, Ann Judson, Adoniram Judson,*

Gerhard Oncken, Lott Cary, Charlotte Moon, William Bagby, and Anne Luther Bagby)

16. Rooted in Baptists' belief in freedom of conscience has been a deep Baptist commitment to _____ *(education)*.

17. Also rooted in the Baptist belief in freedom of conscience has been Baptist advocacy for _____ *(social justice)*. Some of the issues Baptists have confronted throughout their history include _____, _____, _____, _____, _____, and the _____ *(slavery, slave trade, ministering to the poor, the role of women in society, orphans, and the civil rights movement)*.

Application

Allow time for members to share their impressions about the information given during this lecture. How should such information increase their appreciation for those who have done so much to establish Baptists? How can it increase their commitment to become involved in helping their church continue this rich Baptist heritage of contributing to the cause of Christ?

A History of Baptists

1. When did the first identifiable Baptist churches emerge?

2. How were they different from the established church?

3. What movement was sweeping through Europe that led to the widespread challenge to the Roman Catholic Church?

4. What early groups developed before the first English Baptists?

5. Who organized the first English Baptist churches?

6. What cardinal Baptist principles were established by the Smyth-Helwys-Murton congregation?

7. What title was given to the group of Baptists referred to in question 6?

8. What title was given to another group of Baptists in England?

   They differed from General Baptists in the following ways:

9. Freedom of conscience and scriptural authority are closely aligned with belief in _____ and _____ _____.

10. Who were some of the most important contributors to the beginning of Baptist work in America?

11. What movement in the mid-eighteenth century greatly influenced the growth of Baptists in colonial life?

    Much of this growth came from what group of churches?

    Who were the two specific people most responsible for this growth?

12. Baptist historians regard the first church founded in North Carolina, whose name was the _____, as one of the mother congregations of these Baptists: _____ _____.

13. The passion for sharing the gospel also translated into another Baptist contribution to Christianity, that of Baptists' fervent
_____.

14. The best known and perhaps most important pioneers in the modern missions movement were these two British Baptists:
_____ and _____
_____.

15. Other Baptist pioneers in the missions movement include these leaders:

16. Rooted in Baptists' belief in freedom of conscience has been a deep Baptist commitment to

17. Also rooted in the Baptist belief in freedom of conscience has been Baptist advocacy for _____. Some of the issues Baptists have confronted throughout their history include

Teaching Plan for Chapter 4
What Are Some Basic Baptist Beliefs?

Teaching Aim: To lead members to gain a new awareness and appreciation for basic Baptist beliefs and to determine how such an awareness and appreciation can be of benefit to this church.

Introduction

Begin by sharing the following statements by Dr. Jim Denison[30] from an article entitled, "Are We Witnessing the Demise of America's Church?"

> Will the American church exist in 100 years? You know about our nation's atheists and agnostics. Now we have ignostics, people who are ignorant of basic biblical truths. Fewer than half of Americans can identify Genesis as the first book of the Bible; only one-third know that Jesus delivered the Sermon on the Mount; only one-half can name even one of the Gospels.

Allow time for members to respond to these statements before asking, *With this kind of indifference to Bible knowledge, what can we expect to be the typical response to basic Baptist beliefs?* This study will remind us of our beliefs in an effort to determine how our increased knowledge can contribute to the welfare of our church.

Chapter Study

Ask members to determine how an awareness and appreciation for each of the following beliefs can benefit this church: (Suggested benefits are included in parentheses. Refer to the material in Chapter 4 for information about each belief.)

Beliefs Baptists Hold in Common with Other Christians:

1. Belief about God (This strengthens our fellowship with God.)

2. Belief about Jesus Christ (This prepares us to discuss the true nature of Christ with those in our world today who have been misled by cultic religions regarding Christ's true nature.)

3. Belief about humankind (This strengthens the evangelistic outreach of the church.)

4. Belief about salvation (All members need to have a correct understanding of what it means to be saved from sin, especially the 40 percent of church members that some experts believe have never made a true profession of faith.)

5. Belief about the Bible (Refer to the quote from Jim Denison in the Introduction to this teaching plan. Many people desperately need help with their indifference about the Bible.)

6. Belief about church (Ask members to recall our study of Chapter 2. Strengthen the commitment of your class members to be effective church members.)

Beliefs and Practices That Make Baptists a Distinctive Denomination:

1. The Bible is the sole written authority for Baptist beliefs. (Encourage a church-wide commitment to study the Bible rather than other subjects in Bible classes.)

2. The Lordship of Christ (An increased understanding of what is meant by the Lordship of Christ in a Christian's life is desperately needed in every church today.)

3. Soul competency (This strengthens church members' commitment to the will of God in their lives.)

4. The nature of salvation (Having a true understanding of salvation prepares members to communicate more effectively with those who follow works-based religions.)

5. The priesthood of all believers (This strengthens the personal prayer life of members.)

6. Believer's baptism by immersion (Leads to appreciation for our Baptist heritage and to more meaningful worship during baptismal services.)

7. A regenerate church membership (More care should be taken at the point of a person's request for church membership. Prospective members should be carefully prepared for church membership by understanding what it means in their daily lives.)

8. Congregational church governance (Church polity should ensure governance by the congregation rather than by a select few.)

9. Freedom and variety (Increases church members' understanding and practice of Baptist ordinances.)

10. Autonomy of churches (This strengthens appreciation for the work of the local church.)

11. Voluntary cooperation (This will lead to a renewed appreciation for engaging in cooperative work with other Baptists.)

12. Evangelism, Missions, Ministry, Social Action, and Christian Education—hallmarks of Baptist churches and organizations (Working together in these efforts brings unity and consistency among Baptist believers.)

13. Religious freedom (To highlight the importance of religious freedom, conduct a study of how Baptists have encouraged it throughout their history.)

Application

Challenge members to determine specific actions they will take related to as many of these basic beliefs as possible. A compilation of all possible benefits could be presented to the church members for their consideration.

Teaching Plan for Chapter 5
How Do We Relate to Other Baptists and Other Christian Groups?

Teaching Aim: To lead class members to gain a better understanding of the importance of the church and denominational entities as an effective means of fulfilling God's will for their lives

Introduction

Share the following quote from an article by Dr. Jim Denison[31]:

> The number of young adults who affiliate with a religion is at an all-time low. While only 9 percent of people sixty-five and older claim no religion, one-third of adults under thirty have no religious affiliation. Researchers don't expect them to become more religious as they age, indicating that religious commitment in our nation will continue to decline in the years ahead.

Allow time for members to respond to these statements so that you may gather their thoughts and understand how they feel about these statistics.

Present the idea that understanding the importance of denominations and churches in modern society may help each of us maintain a commitment to such entities and the role they play in helping us to fulfill God's purpose for our lives.

Chapter Study

Begin with a discussion of the following question: *Why is building relationships with other Christians important for new believers and new church members?* Suggested answers should include the following:

1. Corporate worship is the most important reason for having church. The only way Christians can experience

corporate worship is to gather with other Christians for this purpose.

2. Each of us was created by God to grow in Christ-likeness. This can only be accomplished as we meet with other Christians in discipleship groups and encourage one another to remain faithful in our walk with Christ.

3. There is a real need for ministry and fellowship through participation in Bible study groups that have these goals as the integral purposes for their existence.

4. God has given every Christian spiritual gifts that can only be expressed through ministry efforts with other Christians in a church fellowship.

5. The only way for Christians to receive the fullness of God's blessings is through the church as it becomes involved in missions and special ministries.

Lead members to discuss the following question: *Why is it necessary for churches to work together?* Once again, the following are suggested responses from Chapter 5:

1. Even as autonomous bodies, most Baptist churches cooperate with other churches through a local association, state convention, and national convention by giving to missions, praying for missions, and serving as needed to support the ministry efforts of one or more of these denominational groups.

2. The association helps member churches accomplish things the local church cannot do well alone, such as starting new churches, training workers, sponsoring the Baptist Student Ministry, camp ministries, and mission activities.

3. State conventions and fellowships sponsor ministries that one church could never do by itself because of its limited resources. Some examples of these are children's homes, retirement homes, hospitals, Baptist colleges and universities, and providing disaster relief. Also, state conventions

assist churches by receiving and distributing mission funds from churches.

4. At the broadest level, churches relate to other Baptists through national conventions, unions, and fellowships. They may commission and financially support missionaries or provide education for ministers.

Present a brief lecture regarding the history and work of the Baptist World Alliance. Be sure to include its goals and information about the six regional or geographical fellowships.

Ask members to suggest some of the ways our churches can and have cooperated with other Christian churches and community groups. Some of these include:

1. To meet emergency needs such as food, clothing, and shelter
2. To address a moral concern in the community, state, or nation
3. To have a joint celebration of a seasonal event

Application

Ask members to reflect on their personal experiences with the following:

1. Corporate worship that enabled them to connect with God through prayer and praise
2. Bible study groups that challenged them to grow in Christ-likeness
3. Specific examples of ministry and fellowship needs being met
4. Assistance with identifying gifts and encouragement to use those gifts in ministry and missions
5. Serving as a messenger or helping elect messengers to attend an associational meeting or state convention
6. Personal connection to a state or convention agency or institution

7. Participation in a community event sponsored by area churches

Close the lesson by reading the quote again from Jim Denison in the Introduction portion of this study. Ask members to share examples of what they might say to encourage the non-religious people of our day regarding the importance of the church and the Baptist denomination.

Teaching Plan for Chapter 6
Talking with Children about Faith, Baptism, and Following Christ

Teaching Aim: To lead members to be better prepared to help children make spiritual decisions

Introduction

Begin with the following question: *If your child or grandchild asked you about becoming a Christian, what would you say?* Share with members that this scenario is being played out in many homes and churches today. Parents and church leaders need help with the most important decision a child will ever make. Providing such guidance is the purpose of this study.

Chapter Study

Present a brief lecture based on the material from the first section of chapter 6 pertaining to the history of the conversion experience of children (under the heading, "Don't Throw the Child Out with the Baptism Water"). Enlist someone to read the quote from Gaines Dobbins regarding the question of when children are of age to make a decision for Christ. Also share the following statement from this section: "He argues not for age designation for conversion, because of the individual nature of the rate of development, intellectual capacity, type of affinity, and environment, but focuses on the understanding of sin and personal accountability to God, not adults."

Lead members to select the best response to each of the following questions, and then discuss each response in light of the material in this chapter, being sure to emphasize the comments under each question:

1. What must children understand before they can be saved?

a. Be aware of the importance the child places on pleasing parents and church leaders.

b. Children must understand that they too are sinners.

2. What must children understand about sin?

a. Children need to understand that they are guilty of sin.

b. It is important to converse with children rather than merely present information to them or indoctrinate the right answer into the child's memory.

3. In what way is the sense of entitlement a problem in our society regarding the conversion of children?

a. When children want to be baptized (usually because their friends are being baptized), their parents often are expected to make it happen as soon as possible.

b. Share these thoughts from the chapter: "While a child who expresses that he or she has already become a Christian should never be discouraged, parents and other leaders may want to take steps toward baptism to affirm the child's conversion. Leaders should take careful steps to orchestrate the preparation and follow-up to baptism. A part of the process can be spending time in discussion and dialogue until a point where parents and ministers feel that the child expresses an understanding of and accountability for sin. This understanding does not mean the child can express it in terms emotionally or cognitively, as do adults, but at a minimum, the child can tell his or her story of confession and conversion."

4. What should be the response to the problem of so many adolescents requesting to be re-baptized after having been baptized as young children?

a. Avoid baptizing children at too early.

b. Make the experience of conversion and baptism memorable for every child.

5. What can parents do to help prepare their child for his or her spiritual journey as a new Christian?

a. They can create an environment where the young child can more easily connect with God, Jesus, and the Bible.

b. They can become comfortable with sharing their own faith stories.

6. How can parents and church leaders construct the best kind of language to use when talking with children about spiritual matters?
   a. Parents should avoid asking questions that their children can answer with a simple *yes* or *no*.
   b. Parents can ask follow-up questions in a way that allows the child to explain abstract concepts such as sin.

Share with the class members some of the best ways to prepare parents to discuss spiritual matters with their children. These include:

1. Provide seminars, podcasts, and other events to train parents.
2. Guide parents to become comfortable with sharing their own faith stories.
3. Involve parents in the discussion from the first expression of interest by their children.
4. Involve parents in follow-up discipleship classes that will prepare their children for baptism.
5. Use resources such as those listed in this chapter.

Ask members to respond to the following statements regarding children's misconceptions about baptism by immersion:

1. Children tend to believe that the overwhelming meaning of baptism is not the symbolic washing away of sin, but the literal washing away by the water of baptism.
2. Many children express that their conversion is not complete because they were not baptized immediately after accepting Christ.

Ask, *Are you surprised by these findings? What do you think has contributed to these misunderstandings among many children?* Share additional information from the section "Talking with Children about Baptism and the Lord's Supper."

Application

Read the Conclusion of Chapter 6. Read the last sentence again: "Take seriously the challenge to join children on the journey to know, trust, love, follow, and serve Christ."

Ask members to share at least one action they have taken as a result of this study to demonstrate their renewed commitment to accept this challenge. Close with a time of prayer.

Notes

Chapter Three

1. Some portions of this chapter are taken from the author's chapter "The Context of Baptist Beginnings: 1517-1609" in Michael E. Williams, Sr., and Walter B. Shurden, eds., *Turning Points in Baptist History* (Macon, GA: Mercer University Press, 2008), 3-12. Used by permission from Mercer University Press, 2012.

2. H. Leon McBeth, *The Baptist Heritage: Four Centuries of Baptist Witness* (Nashville: Broadman Press, 1987), 36-37, and Charles Deweese, "Baptist Beginnings and the Turn toward a Believer's Church," in Michael E. Williams, Sr. and Walter B. Shurden, eds. *Turning Points in Baptist History* (Macon, GA: Mercer University Press, 2008), 14-15.

3. McBeth, *The Baptist Heritage*, 38-39, and Thomas Helwys, *The Mistery of Iniquity* in H. Leon McBeth, *A Sourcebook for Baptist Heritage* (Nashville: Broadman Press, 1990), 72.

4. McBeth, *The Baptist Heritage*, 39.

5. McBeth, *The Baptist Heritage*, 39-40, 83, 85.

6. W. Loyd Allen, "The Turn toward Believer's Baptism by Immersion," in Michael E. Williams, Sr., and Walter B. Shurden, eds., *Turning Points in Baptist History* (Macon: GA: Mercer University Press, 2008), 37-40; William Lumpkin, *Baptist Confessions of* Faith (Valley Forge, PA: Judson Press, 1959), 167; McBeth, *The Baptist Heritage*, 66-69; and Fisher Humphreys, "The Turn toward Public Theology," in *Turning Points in Baptist History* (Macon, GA: Mercer University Press, 2008), 57-58.

7. McBeth, *The Baptist Heritage*, 132-135.

8. Walter B. Shurden, "Baptist Freedom and the Turn toward a Free Conscience: 1612/1652," in Michael E. Williams, Sr. and Walter B. Shurden, eds., *Turning Points in Baptist History* (Macon: GA: Mercer University Press, 2008), 31.

9. McBeth, *The Baptist Heritage*, 227-35, and Walter B. Shurden, "The Southern Baptist Synthesis: Is It Cracking?," *Baptist History & Heritage*, April 1981, 2-11.

10. Mark Noll, *A History of Christianity in the United States and Canada* (Grand Rapids, MI: W. B. Eerdmans Publishing Company, 1992), 131.

11. Andrew Fuller, *The Gospel Worthy of All Acceptation*, in H. Leon McBeth, *A Sourcebook for Baptist Heritage* (Nashville: Broadman Press, 1990), 133-135; William Carey, *An Enquiry* in H. Leon McBeth, *A Sourcebook for Baptist Heritage* (Nashville: Broadman Press, 1990), 133-138; Rosalie Beck, "Baptist Missions and the Turn toward Global Responsibility: 1792," in Michael E. Williams, Sr., and Walter B. Shurden, eds., *Turning Points in Baptist History* (Macon, GA: Mercer University Press, 2008), 102-113; and Carol Crawford Holcomb, "Baptist Missions and the Turn toward National Denominational Organizations: The Baptist Missionary Society and the Triennial Convention, 1792-1812," in Michael E. Williams, Sr., and Walter B. Shurden, eds., *Turning Points in Baptist History* (Macon, GA: Mercer University Press, 2008), 114-126.

12. McBeth, *The Baptist Heritage*, 193-94, 235-39, and William H. Brackney, "Baptists Turn toward Education: 1764," in Michael E. Williams, Sr., and Walter B. Shurden, eds., *Turning Points in Baptist History* (Macon, GA: Mercer University Press, 2008), 128-139. See also William H. Brackney, *Congregation and Campus: North American Baptists in Higher Education* (Macon, GA: Mercer University Press, 2008).

13. Abraham Booth, *Commerce in Human Species*, in McBeth, *Sourcebook*, 138-141; McBeth, *The Baptist Heritage,* 300-01; and Bill J. Leonard, *Baptist Ways: A History* (Valley Forge, PA: Judson Press, 2003), 187-188.

14. E. Glenn Hinson, "Baptists and the Social Gospel and the Turn to Social Justice, 1898-1917," in Michael E. Williams, Sr., and Walter B. Shurden, eds., *Turning Points in Baptist History* (Macon, GA: Mercer University Press, 2008), 235-247.

15. See Keith Harper, *The Quality of Mercy: Southern Baptists and Social Christianity, 1890-1920* (Tuscaloosa: The University of Alabama Press, 1996).

16. Pam R. Durso and Keith E. Durso, *The Story of Baptists in the United States* (Brentwood, TN: The Baptist History and Heritage Society, 2006), 199-201.

17. Durso and Durso, 202-204.

Chapter Six

18. Thomas Sanders, "The Kingdom of God Belongs to Such as These: Exploring the Conversion Experiences of Baptist Children" (Doctoral dissertation, Dallas Baptist University, 2009)

19. Leon McBeth, *The Baptist Heritage* (Nashville, TN: Broadman Press, 1987), 21-39.

20. Clifford Ingle, *Children and Conversion* (Nashville, TN: Broadman Press, 1970), 11-18.

21. W. A. Criswell, "Criswell says child should be junior age before baptized," *Baptist Standard* 81, no. 21 (1969): 4.

22. "Problems Related to New Testament Teachings", ed. Clifford Ingle, *Children and Conversion* (Nashville, TN: Broadman Press, 1970), 55-70.

23. Gaines Dobbins, *Winning the Children* (Nashville, TN: Broadman Press, 1953), 26.

24. Jean I. Clarke, David Bredehoft, and Connie Dawson, *How Much is Enough?* (New York: Marlowe & Company, 2004), 4.

25. M. Wingfield, "60 percent of baptisms are rebaptisms," *Western Recorder* 169 (1995):14.

26. Sofia Cavalletti, *The Religious Potential of the Child* (New York: Paulist Press, 1983); David Hay and Rebecca Nye, *The Spirit of the Child* (London: Jessica Kingsley Publishers, 2006).

27. Albert Bandura, *Social Learning Theory* (Englewood Cliffs, N.J.: Prentice Hall, 1977).

28. J. L. Garrett, Jr., "The Theology and Practice of Baptism: A Southern Baptist view," *Southwestern Journal of Theology* 28, no. 2 (1986): 65-72; B. J. Leonard, *Once Saved, Almost Saved: Revisiting Baptists and Conversion,* Paper presented at Parchman Lecture II at Baylor University, Waco, TX (2008, October).

29. McBeth, *The Baptist Heritage,* 21-39.

30. Dr. Denison is president, Denison Forum on Truth and Culture, and theologian-in-residence, Baptist General Convention of Texas. See www.denisonforum.org for additional information.

31. Dr. Denison is president, Denison Forum on Truth and Culture, and theologian-in-residence, Baptist General Convention of Texas.